Service Dog Training Guide

...tep-by-Step Program With All the Fundamentals, Tricks, and Secrets you Need to Get Started Training your Own Service Dog (2022 Crash Course for Beginners)

Vivian Howe

TABLE OF CONTENTS

INTRODUCTION

If you've ever met a service dog, you understand how unique these companions are. They guide and protect, as well as lead and follow. A service dog frequently becomes a best friend in a mutually beneficial relationship. Maybe you've always been curious about how service dogs are trained for their specialized tasks, or maybe you're in a situation where you or someone you care about could benefit from service dog interaction. You could have arrived here in a variety of ways, but something within you has sparked a desire to work more closely with animals and foster closer relationships between animals and humans.

These amazing and loving animals will enrich your life in unimaginable ways. Whether you are disabled, a potential trainer, or simply a dog lover, this book will teach you everything you need to know about service dogs. Much of the information also applies to other service animals. In many cases, the information is applicable to all pet dogs.

This book will provide you with a better understanding of service dog etiquette and laws, professional training terminology, and the mental and physical tools you'll need to succeed in this endeavor. I've organized the book in stages of progression. It is critical not to skip any steps in the process and to lay a solid foundation for your personalized service dog.

Enjoy!

CHAPTER 1

Introduction to Dog Training and Service Dog Training

A service dog is a canine that has been specifically trained to perform physical tasks or work for a disabled person. This training covers a wide range of disabilities, including vision, hearing, and mobility issues. It can also address seizure alerts, adhere to the person's protection during the episode, and participate in the revival techniques. These dogs require individualized training, which means they are trained to meet the needs of a single person. Training can be provided by the disabled person or by a professional organization and trainer. At this time, no special licensing or certification is required. They are not required to wear outerwear or carry any special signage. They aren't even considered house pets.

Assistance Dog - This is a broader term that includes the majority of the other working dog categories. Essentially, this type of dog assists with various life functions. They are trained to direct, signal, and/or perform physical tasks for their owner. These tasks frequently include retrieving household items, such as cell phones, dropped items, or misplaced items. This term also refers to seizure-alert dogs as well as dogs used in the treatment of psychiatric or psychological disorders.

Guide Dog - This is the most literal term and refers to visually impaired people who require assistance in navigating their surroundings. Normally, these animals are formally trained for guide (Seeing Eye) dogs by an accredited institution.

Therapy dogs, unlike the other three types of dogs mentioned, are not protected under federal law (ADA). You ought to,

Check the state laws in which you live, however, as some states have granted dogs additional rights within their borders. These dogs are considered pets who provide emotional support and well-being to others but are not associated with any specific physical or life support functions. These sweet animals are frequently taken to hospitals or nursing homes. They can bring comfort to the sick and companionship to senior citizens who are confined to their homes.

There is one more distinction, which is usually the source of the most confusion. Emotional assistance dogs are not technically therapy dogs. Therapy dogs provide emotional support in the short term. An emotional assistance dog is considered necessary for an emotionally impaired person to function on a daily basis. As a result, an emotional assistance dog is protected by the Fair Housing Act, allowing a person to own one even where "no dog" policies apply.

Who Is Eligible for a Service Dog?

A service dog is available to anyone with a disability. As a result, the question is, "Is this condition a disability?" This may sound amusing in a broad sense to those suffering from a disability, but it is important to remember that disabilities are legal issues, not medical ones. A report detailing a diagnosis from a physician, psychologist, or psychiatrist is very good evidence, but it is not the final determination. Federal and state regulations will ultimately determine who is eligible to receive a service dog legally.

The process governed by the Social Security Administration in the United States is an excellent example. Most of us have seen one of numerous commercials and advertisements featuring an attorney who will represent a person seeking social security disability benefits.

To elaborate on that point, many people receiving social security insurance (SSI) would be unable to legally qualify for service animal assistance.

The key term in the preceding definition is "substantially limits." If what is commonly considered a disability can be corrected or avoided by taking medication or other forms of assistance, it is not a disability under the law. Assume you have poor vision and would like a guide dog to assist you in moving from place to place. If a pair of glasses or contact lenses correct your vision to an acceptable level, you are not considered disabled and thus do not qualify for a service dog.

Another qualifying factor is what the ADA calls a "major life activity." "Major life activities" are typically those that have an impact on one's breathing, walking, thinking, seeing, or hearing. The best explanation for this could be that an individual would be unable to get through the day without the assistance of a service dog. Opening doors, walking, and sending alert signals are just a few examples. Making life easier or more comfortable is not included. The law may appear harsh, but strict guidelines must be established to prevent abuse and slanted interpretations.

The ADA was revised in 2010 to clarify what constitutes a disability. It goes on to list several physical and mental brain and body conditions that may entitle one to use a service dog. These disorders include, but are not limited to, any ailments or illnesses affecting the cardiovascular system, neurological system, respiratory system, muscle and skeletal system, and other special sense organs.

Under the right circumstances, the mentally challenged, as well as all forms of mental illness and emotional issues, can all be considered disabilities.

There are numerous other diseases that may require the assistance of a service dog. Cancer, cerebral palsy, epilepsy, multiple sclerosis, and muscular dystrophy are among them. Diabetes, alcoholism, and drug addictions can all fall into this category and, in some cases, qualify for service animal assistance.

Age, race, and sexual orientation have no bearing on one's disability status, nor do they qualify for the use of a service dog.

To summarize, the standards for who qualifies for a service dog are largely open to interpretation and are a legal issue that must meet the specified criteria as set forth by federal and state laws. As previously stated, disabilities are legal issues rather than medical ones. Federal and state regulations will ultimately determine who is eligible to receive a service dog legally.

How to Get a Service Dog That Has Already Been Trained

So you've decided to go ahead with the purchase of a professionally trained service dog. The next question is, where can I get one? What are the available options?

While there are dog trainers who work on an individual basis, sometimes out of their homes, the importance of this addition to your household makes this the least preferred choice unless you are familiar with their work or can verify strong references. Because there are numerous recognized, professional organizations that provide dogs trained in programs to assist the disabled, these critical circumstances should make these organizations the first choice. As you look for these organizations, you will discover how many options are available to you. Advertising, magazine and news articles, and internet marketing all expose a variety of institutions devoted to the training and subsequent sale of these animals.

Priority should be given to the quality of education, training, and care that these dogs have received. Another factor to consider is the training center's geographical location in relation to where you live, as well as the ease of returning to them for future additional assistance if needed. Do your homework! Investigate their background and follow up on at least three references provided by the institution. When browsing the internet, don't base your decision on the appearance, popularity, or content of a website. Make an appointment to visit the school. You want to bring home a good service dog, not a good website.

Take the time to go to the training site. The grounds do not have to be perfect, and if used frequently, they should not be. Training dogs can be hard on the grass and the training equipment. However, the areas should be neat, clean, and well-kept. You will be able to tell whether or not this is the type of place where you can count on getting a quality service dog by paying attention to the dogs that are currently housed there. Are they wagging their tails? Do their coats appear brushed and gleaming? Are their toes trimmed? They must be delighted to see you! Even happier to see the handler with you in the kennel. Any sign of a dog in distress or shying away from the handler may indicate mistreatment. During your stay, you should keep a close eye on the surroundings and the residents, both human and canine.

One indicator of a training facility's credibility is how interested they are in you and your situation, as opposed to only attempting to sell their services. Professional training facilities will always require you to fill out multiple forms outlining the nature of your disability, along with letters from attending physicians. They will be interested in knowing where you live. A reputable organization will be concerned not only about you, but also about the dog. They will want to ensure that the dog is placed in a suitable environment. This information is required to ensure that the animal's breed and size are appropriate for the disabled individual's specific needs and lifestyle.

Before making a commitment to a particular school, you should ask questions about the specific training methods and insist on interviewing the specific person who trained, or will be training, the actual dog you will be obtaining. If you do not receive prompt, direct responses to your questions, this may raise concerns about their credibility. In the following section of this handbook, we will go over training in detail.

Request to see the potential canine candidate's health record, including birth information, the parent's background, and the background of any other litter members. If they claim that this documentation is not available, you should continue your search elsewhere. Their policy should be that you can observe the dog's progress at any time, without making an appointment. If an organization does not allow unannounced visits, this is probably not the place for you.

One final piece of advice: a professionally run business will have a rating and any complaints filed with the local Better Business Bureau. To ensure accuracy, locate the nearest Bureau office in relation to the training firm's address rather than your own. You can find this information at www.bbb.org.

How to Raise Your Own Service Dog

Training a service dog is similar to training any other canine. His or her presence in your home will be similar to that of any other lovable creature with whom you share your living space. You will want to focus on certain areas involving their social skills to prepare them for assisting a disabled individual in public. There are also specific criteria to consider when selecting a pet to use as a service dog.

Let's start with the selection procedure. First and foremost, you must decide how you will obtain the dog. Do you prefer purebred dogs?

Do you prefer buying from a breeder, or do you prefer rescue or adoption? This is entirely your choice. Where you get the pet has nothing to do with whether or not they will make a good service dog. Many people prefer to purchase a pet from a breeder or pet store because the animal's lineage is usually available and the buyer feels more confident that they are getting a healthy specimen that has been well cared for since birth. When choosing between rescue and adoption, the other side of the argument demonstrates compassion for dogs in need of a loving home. A dog from an adoption or rescue organization is usually less expensive, though many of them will ask for, and sometimes require, a donation before releasing the pet to a new home. Always consider the additional costs associated with keeping your new addition in your home. Feeding and caring for them will incur costs over time. Whatever path you choose, let's take a look at the criteria for service dogs mentioned earlier in this section. Size is one of the most important considerations. Unless your dog will be required to perform strength tasks, such as pulling a wheelchair, a small to medium-sized dog is likely to be the best choice. While many large breeds, such as the German shepherd, have performed admirably, particularly as guide dogs for the blind, a more compact model is much easier to maneuver through public places. For most service dog applications, a smaller animal is preferable due to space constraints. Consider yourself in public, and let's use a restaurant as an example. It is much easier to navigate aisles and find a comfortable, out-of-the-way spot for your companion to sit or lay if he or she requires less space.

In general, if the potential service dog has a calm demeanor as part of their nature, they may be more successful over time. While much can be accomplished during the training period, it is critical that your pet is not overly nervous and does not react negatively to loud noises or sudden movements. Barking is frowned upon, unless it is used as an emergency alert message. The animal should also be socialized enough to feel comfortable in a crowd and with a wide range of people Age, race, gender, and even the various types of clothing people wear should all be considered. The dog must be trained so that none of the above categories upset them in any way.

While most dog breeds can help the disabled, retrievers and terriers have proven to be very popular in this arena based on the size and disposition preferences mentioned above. Along with German Shepherds, which are somewhat large, Golden Retrievers and

Labrador Retrievers appear to thrive as guide and hearing dogs. Popular seizure-alert dog breeds include the German shepherd and Golden Retriever, as well as a Setter mixed breed and Border collie and Samoyed canine crosses. Therapy dogs, which are classified differently, can be almost any breed or size of dog. The emotional bond formed between the animal and their human companion is the most important aspect.

The First Steps in Service Dog Training

Home nurturing is the first step in training a service dog, whether you intend to do it yourself or hire a professional to do it for you. This stage will be similar to that of any other puppy. There are a few instances where a service dog's behavior should be highlighted more than that of a pet. I'll point these out as we get to them later in this section.

The usual forms of teaching and disciplining the animal, such as "house breaking," must be satisfactorily completed from day one before he or she is ready for continued training. This will take time, and your pet will not be ready for advanced training until they are at least six months old, and possibly up to twelve months old.

Exposure to humans is one of the areas mentioned earlier as being important in the rearing of a puppy intended to be used as a service dog. You should surround this puppy with people of various ages, ethnicities, and even personalities to the greatest extent possible. The more diverse your new pet's age, gender, and ethnicity, the better its chances of success as a service dog. Babies, teenagers, middle-aged people, and senior citizens should be divided into age groups. If possible, you should have black, white, Hispanic, and Asian people spend time with your training candidate. Even different types of clothing can influence how the animal behaves in public. Even exposing them to other animals, particularly other canines, should aid in their development.

Another difference between training a potential service dog and a domesticated "home dog" is having them spend time in and around public places. Keep in mind that a service dog in training has the same legal rights as a certified service dog when it comes to public accessibility. So take them to the grocery store, the mall, and even the movies. Include them when you go out to your favorite restaurant to eat. Allow them to accompany you on a vacation if the opportunity arises, whether by bus, plane, train, or automobile.

Otherwise, treat them as you would any other wonderful little creature. Love them, feed them, give them treats and chewable bones, and don't forget to play with them as you would any other rambunctious, friendly pup. They will find their favorite sleeping spot and take afternoon naps. Even as it is being trained to perform tasks for the disabled individual it will eventually assist, this wonderful animal will grow to be a loving member of your family.

Owner vs. Professional Training

Owner-trained dogs and professionally trained dogs can both be successful service dogs. Assuming the owner is training his own pet and has done the necessary research, the differences are more a matter of personal preference than of quality.

For example, if the disabled person has multiple difficulties, a licensed dog trainer will most likely want to focus on just one deficiency. Normally, the trainer is taught to concentrate on a specific task, a single disability as part of their education. It could also be as simple as someone who already owns a dog and wants to convert it to a service dog for themselves or a family member if the need arises. When purchasing a puppy, the owner may wish to be the one to nurture the small creature from infancy through the training process.

A potential pitfall in training your own service dog is that if the dog fails to meet the training standards, you must make the difficult decision of keeping them as a pet while moving on to another dog to train in the service arena or abandoning the idea entirely. When a service dog is professionally trained, the eventual owner is not introduced to the animal until they are well into the training process and have, for the most part, reached the point where their status is no longer a question mark. Another advantage is that many of these organizations breed their own dogs, which can be genetically groomed even before birth to fit a specific model as a service dog with a specific purpose. Their ancestors are known, and they are raised from birth according to very strict guidelines with the goal of fulfilling the role of a service animal.

While there are many effective service dogs trained by owners, those trained by experts have a higher success rate. Another advantage of privately trained dogs is the ability to choose from a larger pool of breeds. The majority of professional institutes that deal with certified teachers prefer pure-bred dogs of specific breeds. If you are willing to take on the challenge of training your own dog, you will have access to the vast majority of dogs, whether purebred, mixed, or cross breeds.

CHAPTER 2

Fundamentals and First Steps

Training a dog can be a simple process. He responds quickly to his name and basic commands such as "sit" and "fetch." However, training a dog to be a protection dog takes a lot more time and effort. Even for a regular dog owner like you, it is not entirely impossible. It is best to begin with the fundamentals of dog training before progressing to dog protection training. Here are a few fundamental techniques for successfully training a dog.

Training sessions should be kept to a minimum

Dogs, particularly young dogs, can have extremely short attention spans. They easily become bored and lose interest in what they are doing. After about 30 minutes of training, you may notice this in your dog. If you notice your dog becoming bored, you should end the session. Otherwise, he won't remember what you're trying to teach him. Boredom manifests itself differently in different dogs. Common warning signs include a lack of enthusiasm for praise or treats, being distracted by other things, or losing focus on the activity. You can shorten training sessions or provide a variety of tasks and treats. A five-minute training session may seem insignificant, but it is more effective than training your dog for hours until he becomes tired and distressed. Consider puppies to be children who can become easily agitated when asked to do something for an extended period of time. It makes no difference to them how enjoyable the activity appears to be.

Training should always end on a positive note

It is not advisable to conclude training sessions on a negative note. So, do not end the session after angrily yelling or disciplining your dog. Similarly, do not end the session abruptly out of frustration. This leaves the dog perplexed as to what has occurred. Mistakes are inevitable during training and may irritate you, but you must be understanding and patient. However, if you become angry, do not stop the training at that time, because it disrupts learning and may have an emotional impact on the dog. Wait until you're no longer angry, then end the session on a high note. This will also help the dog not be afraid of training because he may associate training sessions with negative emotions.

Set aside a specific time for training

When you set aside the same time every day for training, your dog will learn to look forward to it. When the session is nearing its end, he will become animated. This will also help with learning reinforcement. Repetition and practice will aid the dog's learning and retention of difficult commands. Creating and sticking to a schedule will also assist you in developing the habit of training your dog. Otherwise, you may put it off whenever you feel like it. There is no one time of day that has been proven to be the best time to train a dog. However, the session should take place when your dog is alert, energetic, and not hungry.

Make use of consistent commands

Allow your dog to become accustomed to cue words and to associate them with specific behaviors. So, if you've been teaching your dog to "run," don't change the command to "go" and expect him to run. Your dog will become confused and will not become accustomed to performing an action when given a command. Similarly, do not combine words or phrases. "Come" is not the same as "come here, boy" to a dog. Avoid negatives such as "don't come" or "don't stay." This is because the dog may only recognize the cue words ("come" or "stay") and become confused if you do not appreciate his obedience.

Also, avoid repeating command prompts because your dog will learn not to respond to a cue when it is first said.

Do not alter your tone of voice

When commanding your dog, use the same tone and volume that you used in training. Some dogs will have difficulty distinguishing cue words when they are said in a softer or louder voice. Your

Your dog's understanding of your commands can also be influenced by your intonation. Owners may use a harsh trainer voice during training sessions but a friendlier voice elsewhere. This will only make the dog more confused. At the start of your training, decide which voice you want your dog to respond to. However, by exposing your dog to different voices, you can train him to respond to differences in volume and intonation. This is true when teaching your dog to obey commands given by others, such as your spouse or children. However, you must mindfully incorporate this into your training rather than simply letting it happen.

Make training sessions enjoyable for both you and your dog

You can start and end each session with a game or some treats. This improves the dog's enjoyment of training sessions. Also, instead of punishing mistakes, choose to reward good work. Treats do not always have to be food-based. Oral praise, physical rewards such as playful scratches and rubs, and giving a dog a toy can all be equally motivating. However, make sure that the reward comes immediately after the dog performs a correct behavior. If it arrives later, the dog will not make the connection.

Allow your dog to be afraid of you or unhappy during training. It is preferable to have your dog obey you out of respect rather than fear.

CHAPTER 3

Service Dog Laws

To begin with, any responsible service dog owner/handler should be well-versed in the legalities pertaining to the service dog community. In this chapter, we'll go over what you, your companion, and the general public can expect from now on.

A service dog is defined as "a dog that has been individually trained to do work or perform tasks for an individual with a disability" under the Americans with Disabilities Act (ADA). Mobility issues, sensory issues, diabetes, multiple sclerosis, autism, epilepsy, and Post-Traumatic Stress Disorder (PTSD) are just a few examples of disabilities. If your disability is not listed, you are still eligible for a service dog if you are unable to perform a function that most people consider normal/easy without the assistance of a service dog. Eating, remembering, seeing, hearing, and standing are all examples of functions.

According to the ADA, you have the right to live with your service dog regardless of the laws of your apartment building or rental property. They are also exempt from any pet deposit fee because they are considered an essential part of your quality of life rather than a pet. Hotels cannot charge you a pet fee in the same way. A service dog is not permitted (due to health codes) in a hospital operating room or a restaurant food preparation kitchen.

There are a few things to keep in mind when going out in public. To begin with, not everyone will accept a dog in unusual settings such as restaurants, libraries, or hospitals. Second, no matter how upset they are, they cannot ask you to leave, inquire about your disability, or request proof of disability or service dog certification. Some of these questions (which may be asked anyway) can be avoided by wearing a service dog vest and/or carrying an ID on the vest or collar.

A business owner or individual may, however, ask you what task your dog performs for you. For example, if your dog acts as a barrier between you and people behind you (which is common for veterans who are anxious about being in line with someone standing too close behind them), you may tell them what your dog does but are not required to explain why. Another example: if your service dog is trained to remind you to take medication at a specific time, you may explain the task but are not required to disclose the medication or the reason for its administration.

Flying with your service dog is critical, especially because one of the services your dog may provide you with on a flight is emotional support. Fortunately, ADA law allows you to bring your dog on the plane with you, right by your side, without having to pay any fees. Please keep in mind that only one service dog is permitted on any given flight at any given time. You will be boarded first, just like anyone in a wheelchair. I've included a few airlines and their policies below.

- No cost with Alaska Airlines

- A visible indicator, such as a vest or collar, is preferable.

- Verbal confirmation of your service dog's task is required if airline personnel inquire.

- Service dogs that are properly harnessed may sit at the individual's feet, unless they are too large and obstruct the aisle or area designated for emergency exits.

- No cost with American Airlines

- A visible indicator, such as a vest or collar, is preferable.

- Verbal confirmation of your service dog's task is required if airline personnel inquire.

Blue Jet:

- A visible signal, such as a vest or collar, is required.

- Verbal confirmation of your service dog's task is required if airline personnel inquire.

- Documentation is also permitted. American Airlines:

- Animal ID card, harness or tags, written documentation, and credible verbal assurance are all required.

Virgin Atlantic:

- At least one of the following is required: an animal ID card, a tag harness, or credible verbal assurance.

Although you do not have to be a professional to train your dog, you must pass a Public Access Test. This is a test designed to ensure the validity of a service dog's basic training. This excludes tasks taught to help you with your disability. A minimum of 120 hours of training should be invested in your dog before taking the test. This should take approximately six months. No treats or leash corrections are permitted during the test. Throughout the book, we will lay the groundwork for eliminating these two factors so that you are not reliant on them. If the dog exhibits any signs of aggression or fear, he or she will be disqualified.

The Public Access Test for Assistant Dog International (ADI): This is a general outline of what this test entails. The evaluator and you will decide on a suitable location for the test. He or she will be in charge of bringing an assistant, a plate of food, an assistant dog, and access to a shopping cart.

- Maintain Control When Unloading Your Dog From a Vehicle: Unload any necessary equipment, such as a wheelchair, crutches, canes, and so on. After that, the dog can be let out of the vehicle and wait for further instructions from the handler. The dog must not be allowed to run loose or ignore any commands issued by the handler. Once the handler and dog are at ease, an assistant with a dog will arrive walk by you about six feet away. Both dogs must maintain control and remain calm. They should not be attempting to approach each other.

- Approaching the Establishment: After completing the first exercise, you and your dog will navigate through the parking lot towards the agreed-upon location's building. When cars or other distractions appear, your dog should not be afraid of them. If you come to a halt for any reason, your dog must do the same.

- Controlled Entry Through Doorway: As you walk through the building's threshold, you must maintain control and pass safely through the doorway. Once inside, your dog is not permitted to leave the relative heel position and must not seek attention from anyone.

- Heeling Through the Building: As you walk through the building, you must demonstrate control of your dog. Your dog should be no more than a foot away from you and should be able to walk through crowds at your pace. S/he must slow down to match your pace and come to a complete stop when you do. Turning corners should be quick and without lag. If your dog is in a tight space, he or she should be able to navigate safely without damaging any merchandise around him or her. The only time you should let go of the lead is if he is pulling your wheelchair.

- Six Foot Recall on Lead: Once in an open area, your evaluator will prompt you to perform a six-foot recall. You will leave your dog in a stay position on a six-foot (or longer) leash, turn, and call your dog to you. This must be a simple and quick action. The dog must not dredge or seek strangers' attention. When you return, your dog must come close enough to be touched.

- Sit on Command: You will be asked to sit your dog three times in total. The dog should respond quickly each time, with no more than two repetitions of the command. The initial seat will be next to a plate of food. You may correct your dog verbally or physically for sniffing the food, but once corrected, your dog should sit and ignore the food completely. He/she will not be mocked by the food. For the second session, you will be asked to sit your dog, and the evaluator's assistant will walk past you with a shopping cart within three feet. Your dog must not be afraid of the cart. If he or she begins to move, you may correct him or her to keep the sit. Finally, while the evaluator's assistant walks up behind you and your dog, begins a conversation with you, and pets your dog, your dog must maintain a sit. Your dog must not move to attract the attention of the assistant. You may be permitted to verbally repeat yourself in order to encourage the stay or to administer a physical correction.

- Down on Command: Down on command, like exercise six, will include multiple exercises with a few variations. You will be seated at a table for the first down, with your dog in a down underneath the table out of the way. Food will then be dropped from the table, and your dog must stay in place and not move to eat or sniff the food. You will be permitted to correct others verbally or physically. Once the second down is completed, an adult and a child will approach you and your dog; s/he must not move or solicit attention. The child may pet your dog, and your dog should continue to stay.

- Distraction from Noise: As you and your dog walk through the building, the evaluator will drop his/her clipboard behind you. Your dog may jump and/or turn, but he must recover quickly and return to heeling alongside you. Any excessive fear or aggression displayed as a result of being started will end the test and disqualify you.

- Restaurant: Your dog will be down under your table, just like in exercise seven (in fact, this is most likely the time number seven will be tested). While seated, your dog should not show any interest in other tables or people as you walk by. Once seated, he or she should not obstruct the aisle in any way. Your dog will be allowed to move slightly (stand, spin, and lay down) in order to be comfortable, as long as they don't need much correcting or reminding.

- Off Lead: While heeling through the building, your evaluator will prompt you to let go of the leash at some point. You'll keep walking until your dog notices the leash has been dropped. The purpose of the test, which will vary depending on your disability, is to demonstrate that you can maintain control of your dog and regain control of the leash.

- Separation: While you walk 20 feet away, the evaluator's assistant will take your dog's leash and passively hold the dog without giving him/her any commands. Your dog must remain calm and collected, with no signs of stress, whining, or barking. Aggression will also result in disqualification.

- Controlled Exit: Just as you entered the building, you and your dog must safely exit through the threshold and navigate back through the parking lot. When confronted with traffic noises, cars, or other distractions, he must not display any signs of aggression or fear.

- Controlled Loading into the Vehicle: Once at the vehicle, your dog must wait patiently and not wander while you load your gear into the vehicle. Then load your dog safely.

- Team Relationship: Throughout the test, you and your dog should be calm and cooperative, with little to no adversity. You should both project positivity to the public and maintain a relaxed demeanor.

It would also be a good idea for you to take the Canine Good Citizen Test. This is an excellent way to demonstrate that you have trained your dog to be safe in public with children, other people, and dogs. This test should be performed without the wearer's service vest.

Canine Good Citizen Test: You may recognize some of these exercises from the Public Access Test.

- Friendly Stranger: Your dog must sit patiently by your side while a stranger/evaluator approaches you. The evaluator will then typically shake your hand and have a brief conversation with you. Your dog should be fearless, aggressive, or shy in the presence of the stranger who will be ignoring him/her.

- Sitting Politely for Petting: Your dog should not show disdain or shyness toward the evaluator while he or she puts his or her head and body. While this test is being performed, you may reassure your dog.

- Appearance and Grooming: It is critical that your dog is visually appealing and clean for places such as hospitals and restaurants. This test not only demonstrates your dog's aversion to being groomed, but it also evaluates his or her health (including proper weight and mentally alert). His/her ears, paws, and gums will be examined by the evaluator. Then, comb your dog's fur softly and naturally.

- Walking on a Loose Leash: You will often be expected to walk your dog on a loose leash if you are given a pre-planned route. Your dog's focus should be on you and the area you're walking in. This is to show that you can control your dog while walking and changing directions. At least one right turn, one left turn, and one halt are required.

- Walking Through a Crowd: A crowd of people, according to the American Kennel Club, consists of at least three people. You and your dog must walk politely through the crowd without putting any strain on the leash.

- Sit, Down, and Stay on Command: Your dog's leash is replaced with a 20-foot leash prior to the test. You will sit your dog and then command them to down. You will leave your dog once he or she is in the down position. You can say stay or simply leave your dog's side if you have built the stay into your dog's down. At a natural pace, you will walk away from your dog's side, turn at the end of the leash, and calmly return to your dog. S/he must remain in the position you left them in until the evaluator provides additional instructions.

- Recall: Just like the stay exercise, you'll leave your dog and walk 10 feet away. You will turn and face once you are 10 feet away.

Your dog and address him/her:

- Reaction to Another Dog: The goal of this test is to see how your dog reacts to other dogs. You and another handler, accompanied by their dog, will begin walking towards each other from a distance of 20 feet. Your dog must not act exuberantly, fearfully, or aggressively toward the approaching dog. When you reach each other, you will come to a halt, shake hands, and make small talk. The dogs may acknowledge each other's presence but are unlikely to be particularly interested. Then you'll walk past each other for another 10 feet. Your dog must remain focused on you and not on the dog behind them.

- Reaction to distraction: The evaluator will present you and your dog with two distractions during this test. During this time, your dog must maintain his confidence. He or she should not bark or panic by displaying fear or aggression. Distractions you may encounter during the test include an open umbrella, a jogger passing by, a chair falling, or dropping a crutch or cane.

- Supervised Separation: The goal of this test is to show that your dog can be left with a trusted friend or family member while you leave and walk away from your dog. During this exercise, your dog must be under the control of whoever is holding the leash. The evaluator removes your leash, and you must remain out of sight for up to three minutes. During this time, he/she must not whine, bark, or pace.

Flat collars and choke collars made of nylon, leather, or chain are the only collars permitted during the Canine Good Citizen Test. Electric collars, prong collars, and halters are not permitted. For your dog, you can also use a body harness or vest. The long line will be supplied by your evaluator. You are, however, required to bring your own brush or comb.

Toys and food are not permitted as rewards during the test. However, you may pet your dog in between exercises. With the exception of the last exercise, which must be performed outside, your dog must not eliminate during the test. They will be disqualified if they do. Any aggression displayed by your dog will result in disqualification as well.

It is critical to keep your service dog healthy and clean. As a member of society, he or she must smell neutral and appear clean. A service dog's nails must be reshaped and kept short in order to avoid damaging any objects encountered in public, such as store shelves. It is advisable to carry a brush, comb, and sanitary wipes with you at all times. Shedding must be kept to a minimum; many restaurants are hesitant to serve service dogs due to owners who do not control their shedding, among other reasons. The sanitary wipes are more important for your dog's health. The world is a disgusting place, and the ground is filthy. It is critical to inspect your dog's paw pads on a regular basis to ensure they are clean and safe. For example, if you were at the mechanics, walking on the garage floor, or even in a parking lot, your dog could pick up oils from cars on his/her pads and then ingest the oils by licking their paws.

CHAPTER 4

Service dogs variations and their functions

"Puppy" is necessary because mutts are the most commonly perceived species as administration creatures. Although smaller horses are permitted to assist a disabled man, they are managed under new and separate arrangements. The ADA defines administration pooches as primarily working mutts who are not considered pets.

"Work or undertaking" implies that the canine must be prepared to make a specific move when called upon to assist an individual with a disability. The task performed by the dog must be specifically associated with the individual's inability.

"Inability" is defined as a physical or mental disability that significantly limits at least one significant life activity of a person.

Service Dog Types

There are three types of administration or assistance puppies. Control puppy, hearing dog, and administration dog are the classes.

Dazzle is encouraged by guide dogs, and people who appear to be disabled explore nature.

Hearing dogs alert people who are deafeningly deafeningly deafeningly deafeningly deafeningly deafeningly dea

Administration pooches assist people who have disabilities other than vision or hearing. This includes puppies who are trained to work with people who use wheelchairs, have balance issues, have chemical imbalances, require seizure alarm or reaction, should be alerted to other medical issues such as low glucose, or have mental inabilities.

Service Dog Breeds That Are Common

Labrador Retrievers and Golden Retrievers are the most well-known breeds for guide mutts and versatility to help puppies.

The administration canine's territory ranges in size from small to large. The puppy must be able to easily carry out the tasks required to help moderate a handicap. A Papillon, for example, would not be an appropriate choice to pull a wheelchair, but would make an excellent hearing aid canine or enthusiastic help puppy. Many administration pooches are gradually rescued from safe houses.

Therapy Dog vs. Administration Dog

Many people confuse service dogs and service mutts, but they perform two completely different jobs that necessitate nearly opposite characteristics.

Administration mutts are one dog for one person who performs specific tasks to help that person adjust to a disability. Treatment mutts are one canine for everyone—they bring joy and solace to hospital patients, assisted living and nursing home residents, destitute families, and understudies.

Administration mutts must be handler-centered, desensitized to distractions, and extremely prepared to perform specific tasks. When working, they should not be distracted by the general public and should focus solely on their boss. Preparation for administration canines can last up to two years before they are placed with a customer. Administration mutts are required to wear a vest that identifies them as an administration pooch and requests that the general public did not pet them.

Treatment pooches should be friendly and cordial, yet quiet and respectful, and attached to a variety of people, places, and things. Treatment canines should be prepared in basic behavior and acquiescence, and they must attend training workshops. On a volunteer basis, treatment mutts and their owners provide opportunities for petting and warmth in a variety of settings.

Making a Service Dog

Administration puppy preparation is a time-consuming and exhausting process. Puppies must be able to complete their tasks on time and must demonstrate the abilities required for the Assistance Dogs International Public Access Test, a series of destinations intended to assess the puppy's behavior in distracting conditions.

Many administration canines are created specifically for the task by organizations, which then train and place them with customers. The associations have high standards, and not all mutts pass the final requirements to be placed with a proprietor. Dropout rates for association prepared administration pooches can range from 50 to 70%.

In the most recent couple of years, proprietor prepared administration canines have grown in popularity. Long holding records, additional time and expense, and the risk of getting an organization-prepared canine have aided more people who are unable to prepare their own administration puppies. Owners who need to prepare their own mutts to assist them should seek expert puppy preparation assistance from a coach who has experience working with administration pooches. They should consult with Assistance Dogs International (ADI) for assistance in finding a mentor and to ensure they are aware of all applicable laws, including those governing administration canines.

Each administration dog must be prepared in entrusting abilities specific to the handler's inability as well as in free abilities. According to ADA guidelines, administration pooches should also be house-prepared and under constant open control.

Regardless of breed, all assistance dogs require a unique set of qualities in order to be steadfast in their work. These characteristics may include:

1. They are usually calm and friendly, even to strangers.

2. They have a desire to please.

3. They have a proclivity to pursue you.

4. They are socialized to a variety of situations and conditions.

5. They are capable of rapid adaptation and data storage.

6. They are always alert but not receptive.

7. They can always be contacted by anyone, including strangers.

In general, all dogs are expected to be cautious in public. The behavioral expectations for service dogs, on the other hand, are always higher. These behavioral characteristics are critical. They frequently include:

1. No coercive behavior toward individuals or strangers.

2. They should not request nourishment or petting from others while on duty.

3. No sniffing stock or people or invading another canine's space while on duty.

4. Socialize in order to endure strange sights, sounds, and smells in a variety of open settings.

5. Ignores food on the floor or in the canine's region while working outside the house.

6. Works smoothly on chain. There will be no wild behavior or pointless vocalizations in broad daylight settings.

7. No peeing or pooping in the open unless directed or flagged to do so in a suitable location.

There are various types of assistance/service dogs, and some of them serve more than one purpose. Potential service dogs are usually subjected to rigorous training regimens before being assigned to their handlers. The following are some examples of service dogs:

- The service dogs.

One of the most well-known types of service dogs is those that guide visually impaired or blind people around obstacles. Labrador Retrievers, Golden Retrievers, and Lab/Golden hybrids are the most common dog breeds that serve or could serve as guide dogs.

- Hearing Assistance Dogs

Individuals with hearing impairments can benefit from service dogs by alerting their handlers to sounds such as heavy alarms, ringing bells or vehicular horns, and even toddler cries.

Labradors and Golden Retrievers are commonly chosen as hearing canines; however, numerous other breeds, including Cocker Spaniels and Miniature Poodles, have been successfully trained to alarm as a conference hound. When these dogs hear these noises, they simply rub their bodies together with their handlers and follow them in the direction of the noise.

- Mobility Assistance Canines

This type of service dog can perform a wide range of tasks for individuals or their handlers who have multiple mobility issues. According to the researchers, mobility service dogs can bring objects to people, push buttons on automatic doors, and sometimes help pull a wheelchair up a rolling stairwell.

These dogs assist their owners in increasing their personal independence and confidence.

People suffering from spinal cord injuries, brain disorders, muscular disorders, and arthritis benefit from being paired with a mobility service dog. Various breeds are carefully selected based on the handler's size, but the dog must be large enough to provide adequate support to their handlers.

- Diabetes Alert Dogs (DADs).

This type of service dog gives their handlers independence and security by detecting chemical changes in their blood sugar level. They do this by detecting changes in diabetic patients that are associated with hyperglycemic or hypoglycemic occurrences. These changes are often imperceptible to humans, but dogs can detect them and alert their handlers to blood sugar level decreases and increases before they become dangerous.

Many of these service dogs are trained to alert other members of their handler's household or to activate a dedicated alarm system if necessary.

- Seizure Alert Canines

These service alert dog categories are typically a contentious type of service dog.

They exhibit unusual behavior even before their handler has a seizure. Though experts argue that there isn't enough evidence to say that dogs can truly predict or respond to seizures.

- Seizure Response Canines

Seizure response service dogs are raised in such a way that they can assist someone who is having an epileptic seizure or any other type of dangerous seizure. They should not be confused with seizure alert service dogs because they have not been trained to predict seizures. During their handler's seizures, they are trained to bark for help or to press an emergency alarm system button. They are also trained to assist in getting a person to a safe location during seizures. These seizure response dogs could also assist in the delivery of drugs or a phone for the purpose of calling an individual who is recovering from a seizure.

- Psychiatric Service Animals

This adaptable classification of service dogs assists people who are suffering from issues such as depression, anxiety, and frequently post-traumatic stress disorder. PTSD can strike people after they have served in combat, worked as a person on call, or have been subjected to maltreatment, catastrophic events, psychological oppression, or other life-altering events, such as car accidents.

Their handlers in this class may be overly concerned about their well-being, and administrative canines can help their handlers relax by turning on the house lights.

- Autistic Support Dogs

Individuals with autism benefit from service dogs in the form of a prediction instinct, as this affects children the most. In social settings such as school, where these children tend to feel good. These service dogs could be extremely beneficial to children who have difficulty socializing with their classmates. In addition to improving the child's way of coping with life by reducing the child's tendency to distance himself or herself from others and assisting in providing succor for the child in times of need. They are also trained to help prevent children from running away and to track them down if they do.

- Fetal Alcohol Spectrum Disorders, also known as (FASDs). Service animals

This type of service dog assists children or children who were exposed to alcohol prior to birth. These children may have both physical and mental difficulties, such as behavioral issues and learning difficulties.

- Allergy Detection Canines

Allergy detection dogs are a type of service dog that is specifically trained to sniff out and alert to the smell of substances such as peanuts or gluten. They are frequently paired with children and sometimes older adults, and they can be trained to alert to allergy-inducing odors at school, giving the children a greater sense of independence and ensuring that their parents do not feel threatened.

CHAPTER 5

The First Five Skills to Teach

It is critical that you take the time to teach your dog specific commands and actions when training him. These basic training commands and cues help to keep your dog under control while also instilling a sense of order and structure in the dog. The simple commands also aid in the management of a variety of common dog behavioral issues. In some cases, a well-placed command can even save your dog's life.

One of the first things a dog should learn is respect and basic discipline, which is defined by basic commands and energy from the owner. Basic training that addresses behavioral issues is also required for a well-behaved dog. Before you begin training your dog on commands, remember to be:

- Patient and consistent with the training

- Never push the dog too hard as you begin

- Look for a quiet place for the exercises and avoid distractions

- Keep the learning sessions short and simple.

- Keep the training consistent and remember to reward the dog.

- When an old command is mastered, teach a new one.

- Participate in the training exercises; try to make it fun and enjoyable for both of you.

- Make it exciting and enjoyable.

The Instructions Command "Watch Me"

While maintaining eye contact with the dog, teach this command. You should also say the words while holding a reward in your hand and moving your hand upwards from the dog's nose towards your face. The dog should be able to see you while you issue the command.

Repeat the command every day until the dog is well-trained. This command is extremely important and serves as a bridge for practicing other commands.

Command to sit

This command can be taught by bringing the dog's treat closer to the nose so it can smell it but not catch it. This command can also aid in the management of some undesirable behaviors.

Maintain command

This command is taught by asking the dog to sit while holding a treat close to the dog's nose and then saying "stay." You can give the dog a treat if it stays and waits. This command aids in the dog's self-control, which is an important behavior.

Lower command

This command is considered difficult because it places the dog in a passive position. To teach the command, you'll need a tasty treat in your closed hand. The treat can then be moved closer to the dog's nose. As you move the treat to the floor, the dog will sink lower. You can then move your hand on the floor to provoke it to follow while lying down. With an okay, you can release the dog from this command.

Command to Wait

You can teach this command by walking the dog to the door and then commanding the dog to sit. Then, while presenting the palm of your hands and commanding the dog to wait, point your fingers upwards. While the dog waits, you can open the door and then close it as the dog approaches the door. You can also give the dog a treat and then let it go by saying okay or brake.

Come, take command.

This command can be taught by placing a leash or collar on the dog at a distance and then pulling the dog towards you the tether When the dog approaches you, you must reward it with a treat. This exercise can help to protect the dog if it gets into a fight with another dog.

The heel command

This command can be taught by pulling on the dog's leash while walking. You can also tell it to sit at some point. Once the command is completed, you can reward the dog with a treat.

Take it and throw it away command

This command can be taught by holding an object that the dog values in one hand and prompting the dog to follow the thing and grab it. When it opens its mouth to pick up the object, you can issue a command to take it. While the dog is enjoying the object, provide another that is identical to the one the dog is playing with, and the dog will be enticed to drop and pick up the other one. You can tell the dog to drop it as soon as it opens its mouth.

Give the dog a command to take the new object as it approaches. The exercise should be repeated until it is mastered.

Off the hook

This command can be taught by holding the treat in both hands and then moving the closed hands closer to the dog's face for the dog to smell and lick. Because the hand is closed, making it difficult for the dog to lick, the dog will back off, at which point you should open the hand and give the treat while giving the command off.

Command "Leave it"

Keep the dog's treat in both hands while bringing one closer to the dog's face to teach this command. After the dog has failed to get the treat, you can issue a command and leave it.

Output command

This command can be taught by allowing the dog to grab one of its toys while holding it as the dog insists on grabbing the toy you are holding.

You can also pull, and once the dog releases the toy, you can give the command once the dog has lost interest in grabbing it.

Bed or location command

This command can be given by holding the dog's leash in one hand and a treat in the other. You can then use the leash and the treat in your hand to guide the dog to the location where you want it to stay. You can then give a command as soon as the dog enters the area or bed and reward with a treat.

Take command

This command can be taught by commanding the dog to sit while holding a treat. The treat can then be moved closer to the dog's nose. As you move the hand with the treat around, make sure the dog is standing. You can then give the dog a command to stand and reward him with a treat.

Command to settle down

With a clicker in one hand and a treat in the other, this command can be taught. You can then use the clicker to direct the dog to the desired location. When the dog arrives at the location, give the command settle down and then reward the dog with a treat.

There is no command.

This command can be taught by placing a treat on the ground and walking the dog towards it while leashed. When the dog is provoked by the treat and reaches out to grab it, hold on to the dog and give the command No while pulling slightly. You can then give the dog the treat as it approaches you.

Proofreading Techniques

This is the final step in training your dog to learn a new behavior. It entails practicing various behaviors in a variety of situations while also using some level of distraction. Failure to proof the behaviors is one of the reasons why the dog performs well in a familiar environment but then forgets the behavior.

They are immediately removed from the environment. As previously stated, in order to comprehend the significance of proofing, you must be able to think like a dog.

Dogs do not have the ability to generalize like humans do, so a dog may understand the sit command in the kitchen but may not understand what it means in the park. The dog is unaware that the command is applicable in all situations, regardless of the environment. Before being proofed, the behavior should be practiced in a variety of settings.

Include distractions and a variety of settings.

When you first begin training your dog, it is best to do so in an area that is generally quiet and has few distractions. Once the dog understands the command and is capable of responding quickly, you can introduce distractions and practice the command in new environments. You can introduce distractions and new settings until the command is thoroughly understood. If you want to proof a command like wait, you must do so until the dog is capable of responding much more quickly and efficiently.

Distractions such as running children, loud noises, and other dogs can be introduced into the training environment. You can do all of this while practicing the wait command. Once the dog has mastered the command in the presence of all distractions, keep changing environments and settings while repeating the command until it is well established. Remember to proof the handler as well as the behaviors. You should keep an eye out to see if the dog responds similarly when the commands are given by someone else.

CHAPTER 6:

Service Dog Training

Many people with disabilities have learned to take the easy route over the years. They train their dogs on their own. This is not an easy task. Training your dog is a lot of work that requires you to do the same thing over and over until the dog understands.

For example, a good dog that is not properly trained can cause problems for her client. For example, if her master has a sudden seizure, the dog may panic. Instead of driving her to the nearest clinic, she may end up taking her on another pointless journey, possibly into a lonely and quiet place.

This is an extreme example, but it illustrates how difficult it is to train a service dog.

So, how do you proceed? How do you teach yourself to train a service dog? That is the entire point of purchasing this book in the first place. Reading is not the only requirement for becoming an all-around good dog trainer. The book is the first requirement, and here are a few other ideas to help you become a better dog trainer.

1. Have experience with dogs.

Perhaps you have never owned a dog before and want to learn now. Training a dog will not be as easy for someone who has owned and learned to walk, feed, bathe, and do all of the other things that come with owning a dog. So this is your starting point: learn to work with a dog.

You may not have the time to start from scratch, so you can choose to;

- Watch dog training videos.

- Go to seminars and conferences that highlight and explain dog behaviors and how to master them.

2. Finish a course

This is up for debate. At the very least, you are not learning to do this in order to become a professional dog trainer, are you? But think about it if you really want to. If you come across a good course, enroll and learn. With time, you will become so skilled with dogs that others will seek your assistance in training their own.

3. Apprentice

This is the best suggestion on the list. Why? You are getting direct training from someone who is already knowledgeable about the industry. You are also learning in a practical sense, as you are training a dog. If your tutor is an excellent dog trainer (and you are a good student), you will have learned a lot in a short amount of time.

There are, of course, other options, such as obtaining advanced certificates. But this is irrelevant if you are not planning to become a full-time dog trainer. You can start training your dog now that you know what will help. Assuming you have your dog, the following section opens the door to the training room, where your dog is.

After you've obtained a service dog by following the steps outlined in the subsections, you'll need to move on to the fun part, this section, which explains how to train a dog.

Before you begin, here is some information you should be aware of. Each of the ten subsections focuses on how to teach a specific command. If you don't have a dog yet, reading this will be useless.

It is recommended that you have a dog, preferably one that is no longer a puppy.

Another consideration is patience. You must be patient enough to observe the dog's new behavior. Patience is required because the dog will not start obeying commands after a few hours (if it does, consider yourself an exceptional trainer). Never, ever, ever use force in any situation.

Before going public with certain commands, make sure the dog has mastered them at home.

Training sessions should not last more than an hour. This will keep the dog from becoming bored.

This training will require the following equipment and tools:

Certain items will be required to train and help your dog excel at training. You will not, for example, punish your dog, as some people do. Instead, you will reward good behavior with treats (usually dog food produced in small bites).

- A pooch palace or crate: this is where the young dog will sleep and nap when necessary.

- A baby gate: to restrict the dog's movement when needed.

- A bed • Toys • Commercial dog foods for easy handling and administration during training • A small bag you can easily carry around or hang around your neck as you and the dog move This is where you store the treats you'll be using during training.

Training Your Dog To Sit

In a few weeks, your dog should be able to obey this command. If you use either of the two methods described in this section.

In general, there are two approaches you can take to teach your dog to sit. They are both capturing and luring. Capturing

- Make sure your puppy is looking at you directly, either by tricking her or calling her name.

- Wait for the puppy to sit before saying 'yes' and dropping one treat.

- Move away from where the dog is sitting after you've given her a treat. She will attempt to follow your lead by standing. Wait for her to sit again before saying 'yes' and giving her another treat.

- After a few repetitions of this command, begin saying'sit' instead of yes. And remember to always give her a treat.

- Repeat this exercise for a few days.

- • First and foremost, you will tease the puppy. Begin by standing in front of the dog with a treat in front of her nose.

- Carefully remove the treat from her reach.

- The dog will most likely sit while attempting to nibble on the treat. When her bottom touches the floor, reward her with a treat.

- Repeat this while using the treat as a lure. Then, after a few attempts and the dog has figured it out, switch to using only your hand as the lure.

- Keep using your hand as the lure until the dog eventually gets it. When this occurs, say 'sit' whenever her buttock is touched about making contact with the ground You can also say 'sit' in addition to making the hand gesture.

- Never force your dog to sit by putting them in a sitting position yourself. You'll confuse and irritate the dog.

How to Teach Your Dog How to Heel

This command is also known as leash walking. It is a necessary skill for dogs who have completed competition obedience training. In this training, it is commonly referred to as the 'heel' command. What you want to achieve here is to make the dog always stay at your leg side, her head even with the top of your knee, while you two are walking in a public place. This will not give you too much stress pulling your dog closer. When the dog understands this command and obeys it, it will be easier to take her into public places and make her behave orderly.

Some people prefer another cue or words, something like 'let's go forward.' This doesn't matter more than the dog actually understanding the command you are giving her. Use any cue or words you like. But stick with just one to avoid confusion.

The side your dog walks is also up to you. It is not a rigid rule that your dog walks by your left, if you want her by your right, then train her to stay on the right. Also, consistency is essential so as not to confuse the helpless canine.

The steps: \s• Ensure your dog has learned to use a leash. Some dogs will not find a leash a beautiful piece of jewelry, so they will pull and bite and refuse to stay calm.

- The first time you are putting a leash, give her treat as you go. Use a treat to encourage her to wear the leash. After she has worn the leash, give her a treat. Now move forward and when she moves with you, give her another treat.

- Stand up and hold the leash in a kind of loose loop. Stand up beside the dog so that she can sit or stand beside you. Give her a lot of treats for doing that.

- Continue the two steps again a few times until she is comfortable with the leash.

- If you have done the above step, it will be easier now. Walk with your dog while she is putting on the leash. As you walk, give her treats at the level of your knee to encourage her to always walk beside you.

- When she runs forward, don't pull the leash. Just turn to the opposite direction, call her name for her to come and continue walking. When she comes to your side again, give her another treat at the level of your hip or your knee as you are doing before.

- Then start to make a treat for as much as every step she is walking beside you. Continue doing these for some time.

- Eventually, the dog will get the idea, and she will always walk beside you. Now that you are successful in your training remove the use of treats and exercise with your dog this new command.

- When you are about to begin your walk, you can say the cue, 'let's move forward,' or whatever.

- Occasionally, after you have completed a walk and the dog is obedient throughout the walk, you should reward her with some treats or anything you know she likes.

How To Train Your Dog To Come

Training your dog to come is one of the simplest things to train a puppy. You will know this if you have ever handled a puppy.

Then one day, you are out, and someone's picnic is about to be ruined by your once obedient puppy, you call her. She stares at you briefly and the go-ahead to pull the table cloth under the birthday cake.

Your canine friend is out of control. This is little you can do. But if you handle her training process properly, you will know how to call her in this kind of situation. So read on and see the things you have to do to train your dog to come.

The steps: \s• Start by holding some treats in your hands.

- Now sit in front of your puppy and call her name. This is a simple step; just relax and call her name. When she responds, give her a treat.

- Do not wait for her to respond before giving her the treats. You should use the treat to ensure the dog comes toward you.

- Put a treat on the floor, let her finish it, then call her name. She will look up, and you will give her another treat.

- Repeat the above step for some time until the dog has mastered answering her name. Next, you will add distance to the treats. Throw a treat at a distance and let her finish eating before calling her name. She will look at you and come closer to you. Repeat the process for some time.

- Do not keep repeating your dog's name when she will not answer. You are confusing her and giving her a chance to ignore you when you called. Instead of calm down, move closer to her and use the treat effectively (well, bribe her, for a start) (well, bribe her, for a start). Stay closer, give treat then call her name. \s• Your puppy is now answering her name from a distance, turning her face towards you at the call of her name.

- At this stage, you can add more movement to the training. Throw the treat at a distance, let her finish eating, and call her name. Instead of waiting at a spot for her to come and meet you, try to walk away from her, and she will run after you. Running is a lot of fun for dogs. When she catches up with you, repeat the process and remember always to call her name.

- It's time to increase the distance: throw the treat to a longer distance but a place where she can see it. And let her run to catch up on the longer distance.

- Alter the location. If you've been training indoors, try it outside. Usually, do this in an enclosed space where she won't be able to go wild if she gets out of control.

Warning

- If you don't have an enclosed area to use for the later part of the training, attach a leash to her neck and keep training.

- When your dog approaches you, grab or hold her. Of course, this is dependent on the dog. Some dogs are fearful and will be confused or scared if you reach for them. Instead, kneel in front of the puppy, side to side, and pat her on the collar.

- When you call your dog to punish her, you are giving her a reason not to respond when you call.

How to Teach Your Dog to Respond to the Stay Command

There are two cues or words you can use to get your dog to sit when you want her to: 'sit' and release.' You can use another word for the release cue, anything that indicates that you are able to move from her sitting position.

You will begin gradually, allowing your dog to sit for a set period of time before gradually increasing the distance of the entire game.

Following are the steps:

- At this point, I'm assuming you've named your puppy and taught it some commands, particularly the command to come. The first step is to teach the puppy the release phrase you want her to know.

- You get to choose the word. Words like release, okay, and free are ideal because they are short and simple to teach the puppy. Select a word now and proceed to the next step.

- Say the release word while your puppy is standing or sitting at a distance, then place a treat on the floor and invite her to come get it. When you say the cue word, you are making it clear that you want her to move forward.

- Continue this training until your dog understands why you're doing it. This usually takes a few days after you make a minor change to the training steps. You'll say the cue words first, then place a treat on the floor for her to find.

- Your dog has finally realized that she should move from her current position when you say the cue word; proceed to the next part of this training. Allow the dog to sit (or put the dog in a sitting position) and give her a treat while she is sitting. Wait a while before releasing her.

- Extend the amount of time you wait before releasing him. Use a timer or your wristwatch, or count the numbers 1-20, 1-30... silently. Remember to always reward her when she follows the other cue word. Don't be surprised if your dog gets up before you ask her to; she's still learning to sit for that long.

- Add distance to the game once you've trained her to sit for that long. You will place her in a sit, take one step back, say' stay' or 'sit' to her, wait a few seconds, return the step forward, and reward her with a treat.

- Increase the number of steps you take backward gradually as you continue to teach this new skill. And, over time, you should begin to change the way you take your steps backward. Do it while your side is facing her and your back is turned against her; the latter is more realistic. Later on in life, you will want to walk away while she remains seated.

- Don't use force; your dog will learn this gradually. So, if she misbehaves during training, you simply restart from where she went wrong. She will gradually learn to sit and move.

- Use the same cue word throughout the training, and it goes without saying that you will use the same word throughout the dog's life.

How to Teach a Dog to Paw

One enjoyable activity that your dog could learn is to move her paw. It won't take long, and it will make the dog appear intelligent while you improve your dog training skills.

To begin, you should teach your dog to sit. If you haven't already, you should go back and teach your dog how to paw. Your dog will be given a sitting potion, and it would be best if she had already learned that part.

- The first step is to choose a cue word, something short and simple like 'give your paw' or 'paw.'

- Tell your dog to sit. Holding a treat in your fist while sitting is recommended. The dog will most likely get it with her mouth. If she does, don't be upset; she hasn't figured it out yet, so wrap your fist around the treat. Keep an eye out for the dog's next reaction.

- If she isn't used to playing with her paw, the obvious reaction will still be to reach for it with its mouth. She could raise a paw, say the cue word, and then hand her the treat. For starters, the dog may only shift her weight in her legs, which is a thoughtful gesture in the right direction. Even if she only moves her paw, you should reward her for making a move, no matter how minor.

- You could use a clicker to alert you when the dog moves her paw. Hold her paw with your second hand if she raises it. This is the correct course of action, especially if you are not using a clicker.

- Your dog will learn it in time. So keep repeating the training until she understands it.

- Your dog will gradually become accustomed to lifting her paw when you are holding a treat in your fist. Say the cue word when she raises her paw. When you see the dog raise her paw, praise and reward her.

- As your dog becomes accustomed to this new skill, introduce new ones. For example, you could change the training location to a noisy location, a garden, or inside a car.

- When teaching a dog to paw, make sure you only use one cue word.

- To begin, your dog will most likely reach for the treat with her teeth. Please do not punish her for this. She'll get it in time.

- Repeating the verbal cue for the dog to respond several times will only confuse the dog. When you notice the dog isn't responding, you should stop and restart.

- If you want, you can use the same steps to teach the dog to raise both paws.

How to Get Your Dog to Bark or Speak

This is another enjoyable exercise you can teach your dog. This will come in handy if you want to impress strangers or scare off intruders.

However, excessive barking, as well as barking when there is no need, is a problem. As a result, teaching your dog to bark is your attempt to control how frequently your dog barks. Most importantly, you must first teach your dog to be quiet. When you can do that, you've mastered the art of constant barking.

You will first teach your dog to be quiet in this regard. Once you've mastered this, you can teach her to bark.

How to Teach Your Dog to Be Quiet

- As with the other training techniques discussed in this book, select a simple command for the dog to learn. Use 'quiet' or'stop,' or something simple and straightforward that pleases you.

- Begin with a situation that causes your dog to bark. Ringing the bell around her environment, knocking on the door, or seeing another dog are examples of such situations. Try to create a situation that will cause your dog to bark.

- Find the source of your dog's noise first if she starts to back up. Look out the window or check to see who is at the door. Return to her and buy her attention with a toy or a treat. Depending on the situation, this could be a toy or a treat. Give your dog the treat when the barking stops.

- Keep doing these things and gradually increasing the time it takes to give her the treat after she is quiet. Continue, and as soon as she is about to remain silent, say the cue word.

- Repeat the preceding steps for some time.

- Once your dog has learned to stop barking, test her by using the cue words in a situation where she used to back up. Say the cue word loudly but not so loudly that it frightens your dog.

- Continue to try the cue word in different situations to help her master the command.

Teaching your dog to talk or bark

- As with teaching your dog to be quiet, you must first select a cue word. This should be brief and straightforward. You can use the words 'talk,' 'bark,' or'speak.'

- Repeat the process of getting your dog to be quiet. This will help your dog prepare for what is to come. When she starts barking, say your cue word clearly but not too loudly. When she stops barking, give her a treat and praise her.

- Now, wait for the dog to start barking naturally before saying the new barking cue word. Say it loudly but not frighteningly. You're teaching her to bark when you say the word.

- Give her a treat and praise her when she starts barking.

Repeat this step for a few seconds, then issue the quiet command again.

- It will take some time for your dog to understand.

- After your dog has mastered this skill, you should periodically change her training environment and practice.

How to Teach Your Dog to Search

It is natural for dogs to search for things with their nose rather than their eyes. This means you're attempting to engage in what the dog excels at. The only difference this time is that you will decide what your dog should search for.

And this is where dogs (and many other animals) outperform humans. Because of this one skill, you've probably seen them used in rescue operations. They can move faster than humans and find things faster, in addition to having a powerful sense of smell.

Begin within the home with the dog's favorite toy. Your dog will use her eyes first, followed by her nose. Hide the toy somewhere easy to find, and then hide it somewhere difficult for her to see.

There are two approaches to take. The initial steps

- To begin, you should get the dog excited. To begin, jug around or perform a few fetches.

- Now, use the 'sit command' you learned earlier to make your dog sit in one spot while wearing a leash. Ascertain that the dog is sitting and watching your every move.

- Choose the dog's favorite toy and present it to her as if you want her to see it clearly. Place the toy on the floor and move some yard away. The dog should be able to clearly see where you placed his toy.

- Return to the dog and use her release word to free her so she can get the toy from where you put it. This can be done in two ways, depending on how quickly the dog learns. • If you notice the dog is heading for the toy, release the leash and see if she will pick it up and bring it back to you. But if she doesn't, some pointers might be useful. Follow while holding the leash to where she can choose the toy After each successful search, reward her with some treats. You will gradually say the cue word or words you want to follow for searching when the dog is about to start searching.

- The most difficult part is when you first start and you want her to pick up the toy for the first few times. After that, make things a little more interesting by hiding the toy a little, not in a difficult place in the literal sense, but at least hidden from the surface.

- To elaborate on the previous step, place the toy in the same location as before, but hide it behind something while your dog continues to watch every move you make. Then let her look. If she finds it because she notices every move you make, give her a treat. If she doesn't find it, restart the process, making the item as easy to find as possible and making sure she is watching your every move.

- You should be able to increase the difficulty of the game over time. Hide the toys in difficult-to-find locations. If your dog is unable to find the toy during the more difficult level, you should return to the previous stage and restart.

- Once your dog has begun to understand the command, you can progress to the next level. This can be done once the dog understands the'search command' and begins searching on her own. Allow someone else to hide the toy so that the dog has no idea where it is, but it is within the area. After hiding the toy, instruct your dog to search and observe her using her nose to find it rather than her eyes.

- If someone else takes the item and your dog does not move to find it, allow the other person to call her name. Allow her to see the person who is hiding the toy; the person will approach you, and you can then use the cue word to prompt the dog.

- Continue training and improve the dog's ability to find items

by starting over with a different item or training.
She is now in a different location. If you've been training indoors, try it outside.

- In the advanced level of this training, your dog will use her ability to smell to find the item, and many factors influence this ability. Air movement or wind flow, temperature, and terrain are all factors. As a result, it is preferable to hide the item downwind.

A different approach to teaching your dog to search

If you really want your dog to become a superhero like the ones in movies, this other method should put her in that position. In the long run, she will figure out how to locate the missing person.

You'll need something more than usual.

- Another person, perhaps a family member, with whom the dog interacts and plays.

- A harness and a long leash (approximately 30 feet)

- A toy and some snacks

You should also be aware that some dog breeds are better at searching than others. Border collies, golden retrievers, German shepherds, and Labradors are examples of such breeds. It is also recommended to begin training this skill when the dog is still around 12 weeks old. She will become exceptionally good as she matures.

- While holding the leash, command your dog to sit. Then instruct your partner to leave a piece of clothing they wore previously on the ground. In addition, the person should leave footprints on the ground, drop a few treats on the floor, and hide behind an object.

- Speak the release phrase to your dog. She will begin her search, picking up treats along the way, until she finds the person who is hiding.

When she does, you and the person should praise him and make a lot of happy gestures about it, as well as reward him with a lot of treats.

- Repeat the preceding steps, reducing the number of treats you place on her path to finding the person. Then, either by changing the environment or increasing the distance at which the person is hiding, increase the distance and make the search a little more difficult.

Try a different approach.

- Go to a public place with a few other people and leash your dog. I believe the dog has learned the search command and will begin searching as soon as she hears it.

- Allow the person to hide in a single location in a crowded area. Place the person's clothing in front of your dog's nose for a second, then say the search command.

- Holding the leash, follow her. If your dog locates the person, you should rejoice. Praise her and lavish her with gifts.

- Add another person who the dogs know to the mix. Then, make sure your dog always seeks out the first assistant. If she does find her, you should lavish her with treats.

Another strategy

- After learning the preceding steps, you will be the one to hide. Allow your handler to make the dog sit, and then run and hide while holding the dog's favorite toy.

- After you've hidden, the assistant will use the cue word for search to help the dog find you.

- When she arrives, express your gratitude by giving her some treats. Also, tell her to speak when she finds you. If you haven't already, the training is in the earlier sections of this section.

- The more you spice things up, the better. You can increase the distance between your hiding spot and the time it takes the other person to say the cue word and the duration of your concealment. You can change the location and practice at a different time of day or night.

How To Teach Your Dog To Leave An Item

Running at things and attempting to catch them is one of the most enjoyable activities for most dogs. They are naturally designed to run and play with things, including the birds in the area that fly on the lawn. Shoes and bags left on the couch or beside it are victims of this catching and playing. No dog owner wants that. It makes us ill and tired. We adore the adorable canines, but not this undesirable behavior.

The good news is that we can fix it. 'Leave it is a command your dog can learn, and it will save you some of her trouble.

The command 'come' is good, but it won't make much sense when your dog is running full speed to catch up to the young joggers on the street. 'Leave it' is more adaptable in this situation. So let's give it a shot.

The steps are as follows:

- Tell your dog to sit. (We've already discussed teaching your dog to sit.) You may want to watch it again.) Get some sweets and stuff them into a shoe. Keep this out of reach of your dog and wait for her to abandon the treat under the shoe. Give her another treat from the treat box when she does. Use a different treatment under the shoe.

- Repeat the process five times more, using the cue word 'leave it' each time the dog loses interest in the treat. Then, gradually, begin using the cue word as soon as the dog notices the treat under the shoe.

- Enhance training. This can be done while sitting on a chair and facing your sitting dog. Put a treat under your toe and command her to sit or stay. Use the cue word you used earlier, 'leave it.' The dog may still reach for the treat, which you will squish with your toe. If she stays seated, reward her with something from the bag rather than the same treat she ignores.

- Improve the training process once more. This time, you will place a treat some distance away from where she is sitting and say the cue word and watch what happens. If she ignores the treat, give her another one from the bag; if she still goes for it, return to the previous stage of training.

- Add some movement to the object to spice things up again. Sit in front of your dog as before, and roll an object, a toy, or a treat between your feet so that it rolls backward. Say the cue word to the dog and observe how she responds. Continue to teach her this step until she understands it completely. Make at least five attempts.

- You should make the final stage more interesting. So, throw the treat or toy a little further and in a different direction. Experiment with the step in a different setting. Repeat this step 5 times more.

- Following that, you should try the training in an open area, preferably near a park. With the assistance of our friend, place some toys along the walkway and begin testing your dog's new ability. Use the command to prevent your dog from stealing items from around the house. If this seems too difficult to begin with, consider using a more private and secure location. You can go to the park later. You can now make the command appear natural. When you are walking your dog, use the command when your dog is trying to run at something or catch something. If your dog obeys your command, make sure you go around with treats to encourage good behavior. Move to a busier area and issue the command. This will expose the dog to new situations and teach her to obey you.

- Begin practicing this command without a leash. Remove the leash, place a treat on the floor, and request that the dog leave. If she refuses to leave, take away her freedom for one or two minutes and try again. • Reward her good behavior with praise and treats if she responds well. You should use the 'leave it' command earlier in this stage to ensure the dog gets it before making a move. It is not acceptable to use the command too late.

- The final stage of this training, use the command in a park when your dog is completely unrestrained. This is the final test to see if your dog will obey you when you need her to.

Keep an eye on the dog at all times, and keep her leash with you. Use the command when she is about to make a move for something, not when she is already moving and hot on her tail.

How to Get Your Dog to Hug You

How about making your dog show affection in our presence? How will you react?

And some dogs - many breeds, in fact - are natural jumpers who will tug at you at the slightest provocation. You can build on his work and assist our dog in improving or hugging when you want her to.

Some breeds respond better to this training than others. If you have a bulldog, a basset, or any other large breed of dog, you may want to skip this training and try something else.

There are two approaches described in this book. Choose the one you believe will be easier and produce the desired result in less time.

The initial procedure

- Kneel in front of your dog and tell her to sit. Your dog should be sitting squarely, not sauntering over the floor.

- Lift each of her front paws and place them on your shoulders. Then, as a cue, say 'hug.' After a few minutes, say the cue word 'OK' and gently place her paws down.

- Repeat this step about five to ten times more.

This is very simple, but some people want something more because their dog doesn't seem to understand no matter how hard they train.

The second procedure

- You will rely on your dog's desire to paw. If you haven't already, go back and read the section on teaching your dog to paw. You will teach your dog to move her paws to touch an object there. This section will be simple once you've trained her to do so.

- Now, command your dog to paw as you have previously trained, and quickly introduce an object that she will paw at. Don't worry, she'll probably use one of her paws more than the other; humans, too, use one hand more than the other.

- The object you are introducing should not be too large. When teaching the dog to paw at the bottom, I prefer using a broom because the weight of the object can still rest on the floor. You can, however, use a toy or a book.

- Let the dog paw the object with both hands.

- Now assist her in completing the process. This is the most difficult part, and many people give up. When you've finished introducing the item to her, gently push it backward and assist her in wrapping both hands around the object or item. Wait until your dog has mastered this part.

- The next step is to encourage the dog to grip the object more tightly. When she becomes accustomed to the object, slowly remove it from her paws so that she grabs at him. If you're using a broom, the dog should be able to hold it steady after a while. In fact, the broom should not fall off too quickly when you step back.

- Gradually instruct the dog to paw at an object, such as a broom. Later, you will replace the broom with another object and then remove it completely. This other object will be shorter and smaller. This step will take a long time, so be patient and don't put your dog through too much stress.

- Once your dog has learned to paw at the smaller object, add the cue when she is about to paw at it.

- Once she has done this successfully, you may proceed to the first part of this training. When she places her hands on your shoulder, say the cue word.

CHAPTER 7

Clicker Training

Clicker training is a scientific method of teaching new tricks to your dog. Positive reinforcement and a clicker or a mechanical noisemaker are used to reinforce the behavior on the dog. It is a popular technique for dogs, but it can also be used for other wild animals. It uses no physical coercion or correction to discipline the dog. So, what else do you need to know about clicker training and why should you use it? Here are some thoughts on that question that you might find useful.

Clicker training fundamentals

If you want to try out clicker training, you must keep three approach steps in mind.

Capturing

This is the act of catching your dog doing a good thing and rewarding him for it by giving him a treat. Because your dog feels rewarded when he or she performs that action, he or she is more likely to repeat it. To train your dog to repeat the things you want him to do, all you need is patience and the right timing.

Shaping

If you want a big trick or something that requires a lot of practice, shaping might be the way to go. Making a vase out of mud is similar to shaping your dog. You must be precise, and you must continue to build it in small steps. Reward your dog if he is doing things that you believe will lead to what you want him to do. Rewards can include anything from a pat on the back to a hug, not just treats. When he or she continues to take small steps, he or she will eventually make significant progress.

Luring

This is the simplest of the three approaches. Luring is the process of enticing the dog to follow you by manipulating the treat. Use the treat as a magnet to get your dog into the position you want or to do something you want. It's almost like hypnotizing your dog with the smell of a treat. This is the oldest approach in the book, but it can still be useful from time to time, so you are free to try it.

What exactly is a clicker?

There's a lot of talk about clicker training, but what exactly is a "clicker"? A clicker is a small plastic device with a metal strip that produces a distinct sound when pressed. It is used to mark the dog so that he or she knows whether or not he or she is doing the right thing. It gives the dog accurate feedback so that the dog can process it better.

The quick step-by-step guide to clicker training;

So, what is the main idea behind clicker training? It is training with a clicker and positive reinforcement, primarily with treats. So, what are the fundamental steps that anyone can take to train with a clicker? Here's an example:

Getting the desired behavior to occur

Use the approaches discussed previously to achieve your desired behavior.

Identifying the behavior

Once you've achieved your desired behavior, you must ensure that your dog understands it by marking it with a clicker.

Reinforcing / rewarding the behavior

After you've marked the behavior, you can properly reinforce it by giving him or her a treat, such as a cookie.

Making the behavior more general

To properly enforce the behavior, you must generalize it by performing it on a regular basis while employing the well-known 3D's: distance, distractions, and duration. You must put your dog to the test in this 3D world.

Behavior cueing

Once you've finished generalizing the behavior, you'll need to add a verbal cue so he or she knows when to do it. Cuing techniques such as "sit" and "fetch" are just a few examples.

Gradually removing the clicker and treats

Once your dog has gotten used to doing the trick or behavior you want him or her to do, it's a good idea to gradually stop using the clicker as he or she does it, as well as gradually removing the treats.

The Advantages of Clicker Training

What are the long-term advantages of clicker training? What are some of the advantages of training your dog and yourself?

Completed the training? It is not harmful to the dog.

Clicker training does not involve any physical contact with your dog, so if you are a dog lover who does not like using force to enforce a behavior, this is the type of training for you.

Improves comprehension

Because you can communicate with your dog using a clicker and get responses from him or her through this training, you can better understand your dog, and your dog can better understand you.

The dog develops an eagerness to learn.

Because your dog is rewarded for good behavior, he or she is more eager to learn something new. Positive reinforcements are intended to do exactly that: encourage your dog to continue learning new things.

You will have more time to spend with your dog.

Finally, because you are the one who is training your dog, you get to spend more time with him and grow closer to him. The bond between two people who are both discovering new things about each other is very strong.

You now understand what clicker training is and why it is necessary. It is very dog-friendly, and all you need is a little patience and a whole bag of treats to get your dog to do what you want.

How to Prepare Yourself and Your Dog

You now understand what clicker dog training is all about. If you're reading this, you've made the decision to train your dog using this method. This chapter will teach you how to prepare your dog for clicker training while also preparing yourself. These are the steps you must take to ensure that your dog is not surprised by this method and that you can easily adjust as well.

Introducing the clicker to your dog

The first step in preparing your dog for clicker training is to introduce him or her to the clicker itself. Inform him about a clicker so that he or she can become accustomed to it. Allow your dog to examine the clicker and become acquainted with its sound. Tell him or her that it will not harm him or her in any way and that you are only using it to get his or her attention right away. Expect your dog to understand what you want as soon as you click the clicker. Remember that this is only a guide, not a magic wand that will make your dog follow you.

Learning how to use a clicker

When using the clicker, timing is critical. If you truly want to reinforce a desired behavior in your dog, you must click at a specific time. Here are some pointers to keep in mind when using the clicker:

Clicks with two tones

When you want to feed your dog a treat, make two-tone clicks by pushing and releasing the springy end of the clicker. Allow him or her to have a healthy treat as often as possible, such as fresh food rather than plain dog food.

During the desired behavior, press the clicker.
You must keep in mind that you must activate the clicker during, not after, the desired behavior. Pushing the clicker after your dog has completed the task will not teach him or her that you like it.

How he or she acted the timing of your click is extremely important. Do not be concerned if the dog abruptly stops doing what he or she was doing because you clicked the clicker. The clicker can be used to signal the end of the deed. The order in which the treat is given is unimportant.

Begin with something simple.
When first beginning to train with a clicker, do not jump right into the difficult tricks. If you and your dog are both beginners, it is best to start small and with something simple. Simple tricks such as sitting on his or her own, lifting his or her foot, or even playing fetch with you are all acceptable.

Once, click

It is only necessary to click once. If you want your dog to be more enthusiastic about what you're doing, instead of clicking more, give your dog more treats.

Keep it brief.

Instead of long, boring, and repetitive practice sessions, you might want to keep them short and precise. Your dog is similar to a child in that his or her attention span may be limited. Rather than going on and on about what you want him to do, a few minutes of clicking every day might be more productive.

Instead of reprimanding, click.

When your dog does something you don't like, it's better to use the clicker to keep him or her quiet than to scold him or her and make him or her feel unwanted. You don't want to scold your dog and send the message that you don't care about him or her.

Do not command your dog.

You are training your dog, and it is critical that you refrain from ordering him or her around. He or she prefers a trainer to a master, king, or queen. You must recognize that he or she desires a friend as well.

When you're angry, put the clicker away.

Do not mix your rage with your training; understand the fine line between the two. If you allow your anger to interfere with your training, you may not be able to succeed and may have more misunderstandings with your dog.

Use the clicker again and again.

Although you do not want to use it for an extended period of time, you can try to use it more than once per day. Repeating the use of your clicker may be an effective way to communicate with your dog.

Have a good time.

Remember to have fun while training your dog; after all, you're doing it so you can spend more time with him or her. So the two of you should have fun, and try to make the training process as enjoyable for both you and your dog as possible.

Take note of your dog's reaction.

After you've tried using your clicker on your dog, observe how he reacts to the sound of the clicker. This is due to the fact that some dogs are extremely sensitive to sound. If your dog runs away after hearing the clicker, try softening the sound. This can be accomplished by wrapping a towel around the clicker or changing the clicker. If he or she appears to be still afraid of the clicker, you may want to rely more on verbal cues.

Making a Decision

In the previous chapter, you learned how to prepare yourself and your dog. Finding out about dog clicker training is simple, but making the decision to switch to this type of training can be difficult, so let this chapter assist you in making that decision.

How do you know if the "clicker" is right for you?

The clicker training already appears difficult because there will be no physical contact and the clicker will be used exclusively. So, how do you decide which clicker is best for you?

There are numerous clickers to choose from, so let this section guide you through the factors to consider when selecting your clicker.

Sensitivity to sound

First and foremost, you will know if a clicker is right for you based on your dog's reaction to the clicker you purchased. If your dog is extremely sensitive to sound, you should consider purchasing a clicker with a volume adjustment feature so that you can set the correct clicker volume.

Size

Now that you've thought about your dog, it's time to think about yourself and find something that feels right in your hand: after all, you'll be the one using it. Find a clicker that fits the size of your hand and feels just right in your hand. If you are prone to misplacing small items, choose a noticeable size.

Functions

Finally, you should think about the functions of your clicker. Many clickers are multi-functional, with some even transforming into a toy or other item. You can compare various clickers until you find one that meets your requirements.

Is this the most effective way to empower your dogs?

Is clicker training the most effective way to empower your dog? What are the other methods for empowering your dog, and why is clicker training the best? Here are a few of the reasons why.

It doesn't hurt.

The primary benefit of clicker training is that it causes no physical harm to your animal. It shields your animal from any violence during the training process. This increases the likelihood of your dog learning the things you want to teach him or her.

Consider how you would teach a child to walk or talk. You don't just force things on your child; instead, you try to teach them.

You guide him or her so that he or she does not stray from the path, and you frequently let him or her choose what he or she wants to do and then let him or her learn from it. That is also how it should be with your dog: you should allow your dog to learn from his or her own mistakes without taking away his or her free will.

Dogs adore treats.

People and dogs both enjoy treats! They enjoy being rewarded for their actions, and it makes them more eager to learn new things when they receive food or love for their efforts. This is one of the most important aspects of clicker training: you give your dog treats for doing something right, and it sticks with him or her, and he or she tries to do it more frequently to please you.

When done correctly, it is simple.

Clicker training is certainly simple for both the dog and the trainer when done correctly, and that is why you are reading this book: to learn more about clicker training, so hang in there and learn more about it.

Respects the dog

Another reason why clicker training is empowering is that it honors your dog by allowing him or her to leave when he or she does not want to do what you tell him or her to do. You respect his or her decisions in the same way that he or she respects yours. Of course, if you do this on appropriate terrain, your dog will feel liberated while also learning to follow you.

Interesting and pleasurable

It is fun and enjoyable for both of you because it uses positive reinforcement. You'll discover along the way that when you do things in a positive way, you get positive results.

Simple for the dog

Clicker training is not difficult for the dog because it gives him or her plenty of room to decide and learn. It even motivates your dog to do the right thing in order to receive a treat from you.

If you think about it, your dog will most likely adapt quickly to this training!

Make a good relationship with your dog.

The best thing about clicker training, as previously discussed, is that it allows you to spend a lot of time with your dog, which aids in the development of a positive relationship between the two of you. Better communication also improves your relationship. A clicker is a tool that can help you and your dog better understand each other.

Furthermore, the point of clicker training is to never force your dog to do something he or she does not want to do: you are empowering your dog by giving him or her the freedom to choose. It is uncommon for masters to give their dogs that much freedom, and now that you have it, you may want to think about it carefully. You will only gain trust if you also give it to your dog, so learn to do so.

CHAPTER 8

Engagement Training

Now that we've covered the fundamentals, it's time to consider training. Dog training is classified into two types: obedience training and behavioral training. The owner should prioritize which issues to address first. This ensures that the time spent teaching the dog these methods were not in vain. This will also ensure the owner's and the dog's satisfaction and happiness.

We'll start with obedience training for the sake of simplicity. This assists us in determining how we want the dog to behave in the first place. Obedience training is a good transition from housetraining because it establishes the best way for you and your dog to communicate. When your dog understands how to follow your established rules, he is less likely to develop bad habits, which require the intervention of behavioral training.

Using Commands to Communicate

This training method aims to teach your dog to obey specific commands. These commands include "sit," "stay," "down," and "come." When done correctly, obedience training makes all other aspects of dog training easier to accomplish.

It also aims to improve the dog's behavior and reinforces the owner's position of leadership. Aside from consistency and diligence, the owner must respect the dog in order for the dog to respect him in return. Positive reinforcement should be given to the dog on a regular basis. Dogs are sensitive to their owners' emotions, so if something isn't going your way, try not to vent your frustration on the dogs. When things start to get frustrating, take a step back and take a break.

In most cases, the dog will struggle to remember what the owner is teaching them in such a depressing environment. Negative reinforcement should never be used because it makes learning difficult. When a dog is called for punishment, it learns not to come when called.

When it comes to training, effective communication and a patient attitude are essential. Understanding a dog's natural instincts facilitates learning and teaching. The difference between success and failure can be determined by consistency and respect. Remember that respect does not imply instilling fear in the dog. Getting angry and yelling at your pet will only make it less willing to obey you.

Introducing the "Sit" Command

With the proper foundation in place, you can now start teaching your dog the fundamental commands. "Sit" is the simplest and most useful of these commands to teach. Teaching a dog to sit has far more advantages than simply impressing people with its good behavior. When you teach a dog to sit, it will not be boisterous or jump on other people. A dog who patiently sits and waits for his food during feeding time is a joy to watch. It also reinforces that you are the pack leader, and the dog respects you for it.

To begin teaching "sit," prepare the dog's favorite treat. Hold one treat above your dog's nose and slowly move it up to the top of his head until he can't reach it. If the dog starts standing up, you're holding the treat too high. To reach for the treat, the dog should be able to lift his head and shoulders while lowering his bottom. When you notice his bottom lowering, say "sit" in a clear and distinct voice. It is critical to say this only once to avoid confusing the dog.

When your dog is in the sitting position, give him the treat and praise him by petting him. Even though this sounds simple, it takes a lot of practice before the dog can master it. Patience is essential because it may take 5, 10, or even 100 repetitions before the dog understands and remembers how to do it with minimal effort.

However, if the dog does not go into the sit position, you should not say or do anything. You should not give the dog the treat or pet it. Instead, take a breather and try to teach him how to do it again, beginning with placing the treat on the dog's nose.

Introducing the "Down" Command

When the dog has mastered the sit command, teach him the "down" command. This goes hand in hand with sitting because the dog must first sit before gradually working its way down to a lying position.

To begin, you must first instruct the dog to sit. Once the dog is sitting, hold a treat in one hand and motion it up before bringing it down to the floor in front of the dog. You should say "down" in a firm and distinct voice as the dog enters the lying position. Positive reinforcement should only be given to the dog when he is lying flat on the floor.

If the dog reaches for the reward or stands up, neither the reward nor the command should be given. Instead, the owner should hide the treat behind himself or herself until the dog calms down and they can restart.

Teaching the Commands "Stay" and "Come"

The main reason sit is the most useful command to teach a dog is that it serves as the foundation for many other commands. Aside from lying down, a dog can learn to stay after learning to sit because they are more likely to remain still in this position.

The first step in teaching the "stay" command is to have the dog perform the sit position. You should give one reward after it successfully sits with two treats in hand. You must then place your free hand in front of their dog's face, motioning for them to stop. After that, walk backward away from the dog and say "stay" firmly and confidently. You and your dog must maintain eye contact and face each other.

After walking a short distance away from the dog, say "come" and motion for the dog to approach you. If the dog comes, he will be rewarded with a treat. You must not give him a treat if he stands up and rushes to you before the "come" command. Instead, return to the first step and begin by asking the dog to sit again. Begin by walking only a short distance away from the dog at first. You can begin walking further when the dog is able to let you walk away without getting up and approaching you. Repeat this procedure until the dog allows you to leave out of sight and only gets up when he hears the "come" command.

Teaching these commands is beneficial to both the owner and the dog. He has more freedom than other dogs may not have. The "come" command, in particular, builds trust between you and your dog because the dog will always know how to return to you.

With enough practice, your dog will be able to run free and off leash in dog-friendly areas. You also feel more confident that if a leash slips, a fence breaks, or your dog escapes, you will be able to bring them back quickly. Teaching this command is difficult, but it is worthwhile and could potentially save the life of a beloved pet.

It is critical to remember that a dog will not always respond to your commands. This is nothing to be concerned about. When your dog does not respond to your calls, it is best to learn how to manage your frustrations. There are several reasons for this. A dog either does not hear the owner, is preoccupied, or is concentrating on something else.

You have no right to chastise them for not understanding the command. Again, as the pack leader, you will need to be patient and understanding toward your dog. If you are consistent enough, you will notice that your dog can respond most of the time.

CHAPTER 9

Methods of Dog Training

Your dog must be dependable in the house in order to be raised as a good and valued house dog. His knowledge of relieving himself outside, rather than in the living room, kitchen, or your bedroom, must be part of his training.

Dogs are intelligent beings, as evidenced by their natural desire not to soil their dens or sleeping areas. And, in order for house training to be successful, you must train him in such a way that he is able to carry this innate desire of not soiling his bed and transfer this behavior to all other rooms or areas in the house. This type of training will not be easy at first, but with patience and consistency, you can house train your dog regardless of breed.

When a dog is difficult to house-train, it is usually the fault of the owner. This could be because the owner did not understand the fundamentals of house training, did not train the dog positively, or was unable to meet house-training demands such as specific needs and schedules. So, what should be done here? Follow the guidelines below to properly house train your dog.

Household Training

1. There must be an understanding of one's own abilities and desires.

As early as one month, a puppy begins to exhibit this inherent meticulousness in wanting its beddings and areas clean. This desire to remain clean can last as the puppy matures, as long as you assist him in doing so. If you take care to keep this desire alive in your dog, house training should be a breeze. Adult dogs, on the other hand, can be housetrained as well.

2. Recognize when he is about to urinate.

Whether you are training a puppy or an adult dog, it is critical that you learn the signs and the times of day when this occurs. When they woke up in the morning, they would frequently relieve or urinate. Within half an hour of eating, periods of play, and at least twice as much throughout the day depending on the amount of liquid consumed Puppies, unlike older dogs, do not have much bladder control and will need to relieve themselves at any time. In other words, virtually any time of day can be used to urinate or defecate.

Fortunately, with training, a puppy at 14 weeks should have bladder control and should be comfortable sleeping through the night without any accidents by 18 weeks.

What should a business owner do in this situation?

Keep an eye out for warning signs. As a dog owner, you must be especially aware of your dog's need to relieve himself and be quick to take him outside to do so. The symptoms are usually the same in a puppy and an adult dog: he will stop what he is doing, sniff the ground, or circle the floor. If you notice these signs, act quickly or deal with him relieving himself in an inappropriate location.

3. The principle of praise

Once you've determined your dog's ability to understand commands and his limits, it's time to determine when it's appropriate to praise or reprimand him. Rewarding him for his efforts

It is critical to relieve yourself outside the house or in a designated area. Remember that the more you reward him for doing a good deed, the faster he will learn. However, just as too much of anything is bad, so are too many compliments. Simply say them gently and give a small treat. If you praise him while he is relieving, he may stop what he is doing and run to you, curious as to what you are excited about. And the concept itself may have been defeated.

4.   A routine is required.

It is critical to establish eating and walking routines in order to avoid or reduce the number of accidents. Maintain a consistent schedule for feeding and walking your dog. The more consistent you are, the more likely it is that he will accelerate his pace and fall into a predictable and regular pattern of eating and relieving himself.

What should a business owner do?

Schedule your dog's meals at the same time every day. This can be done three times per day for puppies and twice per day for adults. You may begin your walking rounds half an hour after he has eaten. Simply put, if you are house training your dog, free-feeding should be avoided at all costs.

Regarding Crate Training

Allow him time to stretch, run, and have fun. Crate training will only be successful if you are unable to keep an eye on him at all times. So, how long can you keep a dog crated? His age in months can be used to calculate crate limits. An 8-month-old puppy, for example, should not be crated for more than 3 hours, whereas a 6-month-old puppy can handle 6 hours of crate training.

A dog should never be crated for more than 8 hours per day. If you must leave him for more than 8 hours due to work, you can leave him in his crate with toys, chewable, and rubber balls to keep him busy and happy while you are away. This is also why crates should be comfortable and large enough for him to move around in. Don't make your dog feel confined in a small crate. Remember that size does matter.

Crate varieties

This is available in three different styles: plastic crates, wire or mesh crates, and soft tent-like crates.

- Plastic create - this provides less ventilation than mesh wire. It can be disassembled into two large pieces, making storage difficult. However, the good news is that cleaning this type of crate is simple. However, for large messes, you'd have to hose it down and scrub every crack and fissure. If you need to ship or travel with your dog, this type of crate is generally acceptable for air transportation.

- Wire or mesh style - a collapsible model would be easier to transport. Because it is mesh, your dog will be able to see everything around him.

- A tent-like crate made of PVC tubing and plastic mesh. It is extremely light and can be folded down to the size of a few hollow tubes. The only disadvantage is that the dog may be able to chew on through the mesh panels.

Bedding in crates

You can make your bedding out of washable materials like old towels, newspapers, and blankets. Using these low-cost and second-hand materials will save you the trouble of cleaning and replacing bedding if your dog has accidents. If he is well-trained, you can switch to more permanent bedding right away.

Crate placement

The location of the crate is also important when it comes to crate training your dog. This formula is used during training to help the dog understand that the crate is a part of his daily routine or activity. This is why it is not advisable to simply place the crate and your dogs in an empty space, such as the basement or the back of your house. Otherwise, when it comes time for crate training, he will refuse to enter the crate.

Gradually emerging from the crate

When it comes time to introduce your dog to large spaces, do so gradually and in stages. You may select a specific area of the house where you will first expand his freedom of movement. It should be a room that is easier to clean, not carpeted, and less prone to accidents. When you start letting him out of the crate, remember to use baby gates. Allow him to roam around the room and praise him for a job well done once he has successfully relieved himself in the designated spot.

You can introduce him to another room in the house after he has proven himself without any accidents for several days. Make sure he is completely empty and has just relieved or urinated before doing so. Again, leave no room for error and keep a close eye on him. Carry him outside immediately if he shows signs of relieving himself in this new room.

Prevention is always preferable when combined with positive reinforcement. Remember that the more vigilant you are, the better your results with your dog will be.

Training on Paper

Even before the concept of crate training, there was paper training. Many dog owners have used this method successfully, and it may be effective if done correctly. However, when using this method, there is a greater margin of error, even before your dog learns the rule of relieving in the paper. Why? Paper training is essentially a two-step process. First, the dog must learn to eliminate only on the papered areas of a room, and then he must learn not to eliminate anywhere else in the room. The problem usually occurs during this transition.

They believe it is acceptable to relieve themselves inside the room because they are permitted to do so in papered areas. In short, they are having difficulty grasping the concept.

To increase the success rate of this method, paper training should only be used as a safety net, not as the end-all-be-all method. However, if you choose this method, you should follow the steps below:

1. Choose a room in which to store the papers - once you've chosen a room, make sure all exits are blocked to keep your dog in that room and not wandering around the house. Then, cover the room with thick layers of newspapers.

2. The dog must continue to follow his regular routine, which includes regular walks, feeding times, and exercise. Most importantly, you should allow him to relieve himself on a regular basis to avoid mishaps on the papered floor. Do not be too relaxed, even if there are papers on the floor. When you notice him relieve himself, take him outside right away. When he successfully relieves himself outside, praise and reward him.

3. Remove the papers in stages - as the training progresses over days and weeks, and your dog matures, you can begin removing more and more papers from the floor until there is only one paper left in the corner. If your dog has already

developed a habit of relieving himself on these papers, even if you only have one, he will undoubtedly be looking for this specific paper in the room to complete his task.

4. It's time to take it up a notch - take the paper outside the house with some scent left on it and allow your dog to sniff in this new location.

5. Throw away the paper, but leave a scent trail outside so your dog knows where to relieve himself. Continue to praise your dog whenever he successfully relieves himself outside in the appropriate location.

Traditional Canine Training

This method of training focuses primarily on physical corrections as a means of training a dog. For example, if you command the dog to sit and it remains standing, consider giving it a gentle choke or jerk on the collar as you push the dog down to sit. The completed task can then be rewarded with an encouraging word such as "good dog." This method of dog training is considered outdated, but many modern trainers may use it with some dogs after failing with the positive reinforcement method.

Clicker Instruction

This is one of the most popular dog training methods, and it can be used for any type of training, including basic command reinforcement, potty training, excessive barking, and behavioral issues. The theory behind the training is that animals learn best when exposed to operant conditioning, which means that an animal learns from its environment in a way that leads to a positive outcome rather than a negative outcome. Clicker training is similar to positive reinforcement training in that the clicker shows the do that what it is doing is correct. Many people prefer this method because it is gentle and provides a positive experience for both the dog owner and the dog.

Training with Rewards

This is also a positive reinforcement technique, but the association is not with the clicker but with another type of reward. Giving the dog a favorite toy, food, or anything else that the dog enjoys can be used as a reward. When rewarding the dog, it should also be praised in a high-pitched and encouraging tone of voice. Both the dog and the owner are encouraged to show their enthusiasm.

Whispering Dog

Understanding between the dog owner and the dog is associated with dog whispering. The dog owner should be able to correctly read the dog's body language and use it to train the dog. This training method includes some elements of correction that are primarily based on the dog's behavior. When a dog is aggressive toward another dog, for example, the dog can be corrected by placing a clawed hand over the dog's neck. As with the wild dogs, the correction mimics what the mother might have done. A study of the dog's behavior is essential for this method to be effective, as it can aid in the creation of a strong bond between the dog and the owner.

Aside from working with a dog trainer, you can also seek advice from a dog's behavioral specialist. You can also take your time and learn more about how dogs think.

Best Environment for Dog Training

Dog behavior is heavily influenced by its environment. Dogs, like humans and animals, adapt to their surroundings, which shapes their way of life. The environment has an impact on the dog's temperament, level of association, and relationship with the owner and other people. Whether your dog lives inside or outside, it's critical that you find the best environment for training. As a result, a good environment should be free of potential hazards such as;

Human medications include: Some medications can be harmful to dogs, and dogs are known to be inventive when it comes to opening stray bottles. Make certain that the dog training environment is medication-free.

Flowers and plants: Some of the plants and flowers that are grown in the home can be harmful to pets, so be aware of any potential hazards.

Food: If your dog lives in the house, it may have access to human food; however, some foods are not suitable for dogs.

Toxic chemicals: Chemicals such as detergents, fertilizers, household cleaners, insecticides, and others can be extremely harmful to dogs.

CHAPTER 10

Fun And Work Games

Now that you know what brain training games for dogs are and why you should involve your dog in them, it's time to play!

The first step is to decide which games to introduce, as well as when and where to introduce them. When the games are new to him, the privacy of his own turf is often the best place for him. So, find a relaxing and familiar environment, and make sure your dog is calm. Above all, make the games enjoyable and rewarding for both you and your pet.

Talk to him, for example, when it's time to feed him. As you would with a young child, you could ask him if he is hungry. You can ask, "Hungry?" or "Eat?" When you say the keywords, he will immediately go to his food bowl. Do the same thing with water, either by asking if he wants a drink or simply saying, "Water." It's the same method we use to teach our children English, and while your dog won't be able to speak the words, you'll be surprised at how quickly he will pick up on the meaning of them all because you're now verbalizing more of them to him.

The Pup Cup Game is another beginner dog brain game that only requires basic skills. It trains your dog's brain to recall memories. Three plastic cups and a treat are required for this enjoyable activity. You can substitute a toy for the treat if he has a favorite toy or if you don't want to give him treats because he's on a diet or for any other reason.

As always, begin by bringing your dog to a calm state with few or no distractions. Place the cups on the floor, upside down, in front of your dog. Put the treat beneath one of them. Your dog will almost certainly paw at the cup with the treat underneath it or try to knock it over. Make sure to thank him for his efforts and give him time to relax. If your dog does not automatically go for the cup, encourage him to do so.

When your dog has mastered the concept of the treat being under a cup and has successfully picked out the cup the treat is under, it's time to shake things up a little. Place the treat under one of the cups once more, making sure he remembers which one it is. Then, slowly shuffle the cups and have him figure out which cup contains the treat. It's best to start with a simple cup shift so he doesn't get frustrated. If he has trouble keeping his gaze on the cup, assist him by drawing his attention to it as you shuffle.

This is a game that you can gradually make more difficult as your dog improves. When an owner's dog has mastered a game, they frequently fail to advance it to the next level. Make sure to challenge your dog so that his brain and interest are both stimulated.

Hide & Seek:
Dogs and children both enjoy this game. Hide and Go Seek is a basic mental workout for your dog because it requires the brain to think and reason. It stimulates his mind and senses, and it provides both him and you with hours of entertainment.

This game can be played in a variety of ways. You and your partner will undoubtedly determine which route is your favorite. You could also play them all.

The first method employs a toy. You can use one of his favorite toys or introduce a new one to him. If your dog isn't interested in toys, you can substitute a treat.

Bring your dog's attention to a focused, calm state. Place him a long way away from you and ask him to stay while you put on the toy. Make certain that he notices the toy. Make it appear very appealing, but don't let him come for it. Drop the toy near you while he is watching and say, "Find." When he successfully retrieves the toy, praise him and allow him to play with it for a while a very short period of time then have him return the toy. If he refuses, offer him a small treat in exchange for the toy.

Again, keep your dog at a safe distance from you. Hide the toy behind a tree, couch, or other large object that he cannot see through while you are sure he is watching. Call him again to "find." It may take longer for your dog to locate the toy this time. Be patient, and if necessary, make helpful gestures. When he finds it, praise him and have him return it to you.

Make it more difficult for him each time you hide the toy. This will put his mind to the test. If two people are playing, one of them can have him turn around so he can't see you hide the toy. If it's just you and your dog, you can distract him while you hide it. Then, once more, summon him to "find" the toy.

This game is popular among dogs of all breeds. It actually enhances their hunting and retrieving abilities. You can vary it by hiding yourself, as children do. Begin by hiding in a convenient location and calling out, "Find." When he does so, lavish him with praise and possibly a treat. Make it more difficult for him to find you with each hide, working your way up to distracting him and then hiding.

Make it even more fun by adding obstacles for him to overcome in order to find the toy or you. You can put up barriers or even hide yourself or the trinket somewhere he has to climb up to or dig through leaves to get to.

Now that your dog understands the concept of Hiding and Seek, you can incorporate it into a variety of activities to stimulate his brain, such as feeding time. You can play an unexpected fun game by hiding his bowl near where it usually sits. When you leave, leave some treats around the house or in the yard for him to find. Normal, everyday activities can provide excellent opportunities for brain game extensions, so look for enjoyable times to play this game outside of designated game times. The options are endless, so use your imagination and be as creative as you want.

Tricks and Treats

Don't forget about your dog's regular Tricks and Treats while teaching him new brain games. Continue to make him shake, roll over, play dead, fetch, and do all the other fun things he already knows. You can even add to them to give his brain even more exercise. If he doesn't know basic tricks, you can incorporate them into brain games because they are mentally stimulating. Obeying your commands is also beneficial for character development.

Remember to keep the games simple and enjoyable. That doesn't mean you shouldn't constantly challenge your dog, but give him a break if he's more interested in getting some unconditional love pats (those that are just given and not earned) or if he's more interested in the family cat than in the game at hand. If you find that game times are more frustrating than enjoyable for either of you, put the game away and spend some quality time together doing something else, or perhaps nothing at all.

It's Time for Brain Games!
Puppies, like toddlers, are full of energy and eager to learn. When your dog is a puppy, it is a great time to teach him, and it is never too early for him to learn brain training games. It will aid his brain development and lay the groundwork for more difficult lessons when he is older.

Puppies, like human toddlers, can be mini-dictators. He believes the world revolves around him and his desires. It's time to put an end to that belief. Brain games for your puppy will help him understand basic commands and discipline, making him not only smarter but also better behaved.

Remember that, just like with toddlers and very young children, teaching your puppy will require patience. He'll be easily distracted, so the fewer distractions he has, the better. He will also be bursting with energy, so taking him for a walk first is recommended.

While you can adapt most dog brain games to your puppy's maturity level and attention span, some games are specifically designed for puppies or less attentive dogs. Here are some suitable for younger dogs:

The Leader Must Be Obeyed:
You may have noticed that your puppy enjoys following you around. While this can be annoying at times, it is actually beneficial when implementing this basic puppy skill game.

Activate your puppy's interest. You can probably do so by clapping, whistling, or calling his name, but if that doesn't work, you can entice him with a treat or toy. Take a job in the yard or go from room to room inside the house, and he will follow you. Put a new spin on the challenge once he has mastered it. Slow down and speed up the game. Changing the pace requires your dog to use his brain more. You can also throw obstacles into the mix. However, there is something in the path that the two of you must squeeze through, go around, step on, or climb up. This entertaining game will delight both your dog and you!

Potty Time: Although potty training your puppy can be anything but fun, it is an excellent opportunity to teach him more than just where to go. When you take him out, make sure to say "potty" or whatever word you use to describe the act. You could also have him do something unusual to indicate that he needs to "go." Doorbells are an excellent tool for teaching him cognitive skills as well as potty etiquette. The bell is placed near the door, low enough for your dog to reach. He rings the bell whenever he needs to go potty. He'll enjoy this new game, and while he may occasionally overstep his privileges, it'll be fun and convenient for both of you in the long run.

The Store Bought Games For The Pups

There are a variety of fun brain games for dogs available at pet stores or online. Some of these games are designed specifically for young dogs, while others are simple and thus appropriate for them. Here are some of our favorites:

Puzzle Balls for Treatment:

There are several treat dispensing balls available that require your puppy to perform an action in order to access the treat or treats inside. Some roll out fairly easily, while others are designed to make your pup work a little harder for the treats. Make sure it's appropriate for his age, size, and maturity level.

Food Puzzle Toys are distinguished from Treat Puzzle Balls in two ways. For starters, they are not restricted to ball shapes. They come in a variety of shapes and sizes, and some even fit together to form a train of puzzle toys. Food Puzzle Toys are not used for treats but for actual feeding. If you have a hyperactive puppy or one who eats his food too quickly, this toy will come in handy. It motivates your dog to "work for food." It's a great brain game for when he's left alone for a while and will encourage him to chew on something other than your best shoes.

It cannot be overstated that when dealing with a young puppy, you must be aware that he cannot focus for long periods of time. Patience is key, and while you want to increase his IQ, you don't want to break his little spirit in the process.

Playing games with your dog at home is something extra special. Brain training games are no exception, if anything, they are even more so. Because your dog feels more at ease on his own turf, he is more likely to learn new games or excel at old ones.

Home brain games include those that are especially beneficial for use inside the home. These games are ideal for days when it is too hot, too cold, or too wet to play outside.

There are even games your dog can play while you are away to keep him occupied and less likely to cause mischief.

Of course, you can play some of the previously mentioned games with your dog at home, such as The Pup Cup Game, Hide and Seek, and The Word Game. Others, such as those listed below, can be included.

THE MUFFIN TIN GAME: HAVING A BALL This game is classified as "fairly easy." However, despite its simplicity, it requires your dog to solve problems and figure things out for himself.

Take a muffin pan and fill each with one small kibble or treat. You can use a small, 6 tin one, or even a 12 tin one to keep your dog occupied for a while. Place a tennis ball in each of the holes. You may need to show your dog the "surprise" under one of the balls to get him to play, but once he does, he will have a blast figuring out how to move the balls to get to the treats. There is no "correct" way to move the balls, so he wins if he gets to the treats.

DOG GAMES BOUGHT IN A STORE: Dog Treat Puzzle Balls and Dog Food Puzzle Toys mentioned in the puppy section are also appropriate for older dogs. Both exercise your dog's brain and keep him from becoming bored or lonely. Here are some other popular store-bought adult dog games:

DOG FINDER: This interactive brain game is more advanced and will truly test your pet's abilities. He must move four dog bone-shaped pieces in different directions to receive a treat. Once your dog has completed this feat, he will be rewarded with a treat and will no doubt be very proud of himself, as should you be.

SNACK FINDER: There are many interactive dog toys that require your dog to solve a problem in order to get to his treat. One favorite is shaped like a paw and has individual smaller paws that can be removed to store small treats. The goal of the game is to get to the treat below by removing the small paw. This is a game for intermediate to advanced players and gives your dog hours of entertainment as well as plenty of brain exercise.

TAG THE JUG: This fairly advanced game consists of a jug-shaped container where treats are stored. It has a chewable plunger extension that must be pushed into the jug and pulled back out to dispense treats. Some dogs pick it up quickly, while others take a little longer.

GAME TURBO: If your dog is looking for a real challenge, this toy is your ticket to some serious IQ development. It's a wooden toy with sliders that must be moved in order for treats to be released.

PLAYING BOARD GAMES: You heard correctly. There are board games you can play with your dog that are enjoyable for both the dog and the human. Check out the variety of board games available online or at your local pet store.

Outdoor Activities

It doesn't get much better for a dog than playing outside with his owner. Your dog will most likely be very receptive to learning when playing in his own yard, as he will be in doggie heaven. Outside, dog brain games stimulate the brain while also providing physical exercise, fresh air, and bonding.

FLIRT POLE TEASER: A flirt pole is a toy or object that is attached to a pole by a string. It is used to train hunting dogs, but it also makes an excellent brain game tool.

The flirt pole can be used to play a variety of games. You can show the toy on the end of the string to the dog, then switch positions to hide the toy behind a shrub or other object and have him play Hide and Seek to find it.

The pole can also be used to take Word Games to the next level. Hold the toy up and instruct him to "sit up" or "beg." You could also construct an obstacle course and entice him to complete it by following the toy on the pole. Along the way, use the toy at the end of the pole to direct the activity and give verbal commands like "sit" or "stay."

BRAINY TUG-OF-WAR: You've probably played tug-of-war with your dog before. This game simply adds some brain power to the classic game.

A soft rope with a knot tied at each end is required. Give one side of the rope to your dog and keep the other for yourself. If you start a light tug, your dog will most likely take over and try to pull the rope away from you.

The clever part comes in when you give your dog a command to follow during the game. If your dog is like most, he will never give up a good game of tug-of-war, so this will be both a mental and physical challenge for him.

Tell him to "release" and assist him in letting go of the rope. Reward him for his obedience. Then play the game again and call out, "Sit." As you issue a command, prompt him to immediately release the rope and follow your instructions. This will not only train his brain to switch from one activity to another at your command, but it will also teach him instant obedience. Instant obedience can come in handy in an emergency situation, such as if he runs in front of a car, so this lesson is not only brain building but also useful in other ways.

Approach this game with caution for the sake of both you and your dog. Dogs tend to give this game their all, so you could easily be overpowered and he could pull you over. However, the game can be dangerous for your dog as well. Make certain that things do not become so hot that he expends so much effort that he pulls a tooth out.

SMART AGILITY COURSE:

Creating your own dog agility course does not have to be expensive. In fact, you can probably get by without spending a penny. Simply use your creativity and whatever materials you have available. You can create obstacles to jump over, crawl through, and objects to crawl under. While agility obstacle courses provide physical exercise, they can quickly become boring for your dog, so mix in some head games to keep things interesting.

After familiarizing your dog with the basic course and having him run it a few times, have him "go" full blast.

Then, on command, bring him to a complete stop. Keep him still until you say "go." It's actually more stimulating to play some music, have him stop, and then restart the music when you give him the cue to "go" again.

Make stopping and starting fun for your dog rather than frustrating. He will learn to enjoy the "stop" and "go" challenge with treats and praise.

AT THE END OF THE TUNNEL, THERE IS A TREAT:

To play this game, you will need to purchase a fabric or plastic tunnel similar to those used by children. Set up the tunnel in the backyard and allow your dog to sniff it and become acquainted with it. Then, at one end, place your dog, and at the other, a treat. While it may not appear that this activity teaches your dog much, it actually does. It allows him to concentrate on the light at the end of the tunnel. Then, as soon as he collects the treat at one end, call him back through for a treat at the other end he started at. You can play the game indefinitely as long as the two of you are willing.

TAG:

Because dogs enjoy playing chase, why not add a classic twist to the game? Tag your dog, and he becomes "it." Allow him to pursue you as you run through the leaves, around the trees, and even up the porch steps. Then allow him to "tag" you, and you are "it." Turn the game around and start chasing him. Every time you switch out, yell out who is "it," and he'll start to figure out what the game is about.

Games with Words

Word games are excellent tools for improving your dog's cognitive abilities. While the Word Games mentioned earlier are excellent beginner games, there are more advanced games to which you can progress. Some are basic, while others are more advanced. Whatever level your puppy is at, make sure you are guiding him to the next.

NAME GAME: Most dogs learn their name when they are puppies. That demonstrates that dogs understand verbal communication. Dogs, like babies and children, learn words by being spoken to and repeating them. In addition to calling your dog's name, call other friends and family members by their names. Then you're ready to play this fun game with your dog.

If you have another person to play this game, that is ideal. The preparations for this game begin long before the game itself. Call that person by the name you want the dog to recognize. Some dog owners address themselves as "Mommy" and "Daddy," while others use given names or other endearing names. So, once you've familiarized him with the person's name, you can incorporate this game.

"Where's Mommy?" sit alongside the other person and ask your dog (or the name of the person beside you). Have the person summon him or get his attention. Give him a treat or lots of affection when he arrives. Then you can tell him where you are and encourage him to come to you. Reward him if he gets it right. Now you can have him go back and forth as you call out a name. When you add more people to the mix, your pup is learning names as well as verbal and social skills.

While your dog may never be able to count to one hundred or even ten, you can teach him numbers with words. Count to three when asking him to get into the car. When you tell him to "stay," count out loud from one to three. Soon, "1,2,3" will be a term he associates with the passage of time. Give him one, two, three treats and, of course, count them out once he has obeyed the "on the count of three" rule.

WORDS OF ACTIVITY: Say the word "Walk" when taking your dog for a walk. Say "Ride" when going for a car ride. Each time you

Declare an activity with your dog, whether it's brain games, a walk, a ride, feeding him, or anything else.

You will say the word for an activity in this game. Encourage him to prepare for the aforementioned activity. If you say "walk," tell him to go get the leash. If you say "ride," have him go to the front door or, if you're outside, to the car. When he completes the activity correctly, reward him with a treat AND allow him to participate in the activity, such as going for a ride or a walk.

Remember that both humans and dogs have verbal auditory awareness skills. It is a special connection between the two that strengthens our bond with our dogs.

Games for Search

Scent-based brain training games are ideal for your dog. Because a dog's scent-ability is approximately 1,000 times that of a human, he has an automatic advantage in these games. When a dog tracks, he does so primarily with his nose, so these brain games capitalize on their keen sense of smell while also introducing some enjoyable challenges.

HIDE AND SNIFF: Similar to the classic game of Hide and Seek, Hide and Sniff involves hiding a toy and having your dog find it. The surprise is that he will sniff out the toy.

Bring one of your dog's favorite toys or buy a new one. Rub it with a scent like peanut butter, bacon, or even liver. Allow him to watch you hide the toy the first time, then send him to find it. As is customary, praise and reward him when he succeeds.

Because your dog is more skilled at sniffing than any other activity, this game can quickly escalate. Hide the toy in a difficult location and have him "find" it. Add some verbal commands once he has mastered finding difficult hiding places. You can also throw in some extra toys or balls, but only reward him if he brings one with the scent on it.

Another way to play this game is to use a toy that you can actually place a tasty treat inside, rather than rubbing a scent on it tucking a wiener into the ribbon tied around the neck of a stuffed animal

CHOOSE ME! CHOOSE ME! : When presented with options, the brain must engage in decision-making mode. You can train your dog's brain by allowing him to choose between toys in order to find the one with the scent.

To begin, take three toys and rub one with a favorite scent like bacon, peanut butter, or meat. Allow your dog to take a long, deep sniff of the toy. Then, place all three toys in front of him and let him choose which one has the scent. He may not "get it" at first, but if you keep repeating the drill and allowing him to whiff the scent of the one toy before putting it down, he will catch on. Make sure to reward and praise him for his accomplishments.

HANDPICKED: Once again, this brain game requires a decision and challenges your dog's keen sense of smell. Show him a tasty treat, then make a fist with one hand. Make a fist with the opposite hand as well. Hold both hands out and let him choose which hand contains the treat. Give him a treat every time he gets it right.

CHAPTER 11

The Advantages and Tips of Service Dog Training

Dog training has numerous advantages and is one of the most important responsibilities of a dog owner. Well-trained dogs are easier to care for, more fun to love, and are less likely to cause damage in the home. Before beginning dog training, it is critical to gain a thorough understanding of both the dog and the owner's behavior. There are several aspects of dogs that one should be familiar with if they are to communicate effectively with the dog.

Dogs are known to send a variety of messages through their voices and bodies, which is one of the things that make dogs so fascinating. The more the owner understands the messages, the better they will understand the dog and how their messages are perceived by the dog. Dogs are eager students, and training can begin as early as 5 weeks of age. Every interaction you have with your puppy is an opportunity for training and should be taken advantage of.

Before beginning dog training, one should be clear on what the dog should be trained to do, as well as what the dog should not be trained to do. The goal of dog training should be very clear, and understanding the dog's behavior and how dogs think is likely to provide the much-needed insight in dog training and achieving the desired behavior for the dogs. What is commonly referred to as poor dog behavior is not always the dog's fault; it is often the result of a misunderstanding between the dog and the owner.

There are numerous reasons for dog training, some of which are listed below.

Learning ability: Dog training provides both the owner and the dog with a common language that both understands and equips the dog.

A dog who understands how to navigate our world.

Freedom: Dog training is more like giving the dog a passport to freedom because a well-trained dog can go to more places, have more adventures, and meet more people simply because they can follow rules.

Bonding: Consistent training exercises create a strong bond between the dog and the owner and aid in the development of a strong relationship.

Peace of mind: Once a dog has mastered the training, you will have peace of mind because you will not have to worry every time the dog runs out that it will drag you down the street or fail to return home.

Mental exercise: Dogs should be able to exercise not only their bodies but also their minds. Although much basic dog training does not require much physical exertion, the mental aspect of figuring out the exercise can be quite draining, even for small puppies.

Training also allows you to choose from a variety of activities that you can do with your dog. With a well-trained dog, you can participate in a variety of sports and activities such as hiking, swimming, rescue and search activities, therapy programs, rally obedience, and much more.

Recognizing Dog Body Language

Dogs are known to communicate using their entire body. The eyes and ears are quite dynamic and can provide clear clues about the dog's impulses and emotions. The way the dog tilts his head, moves his legs, his torso, or even wags and drops his tail all contribute to the messages he is sending. Body language is a nonverbal or silent mode of communication, and understanding it can be extremely beneficial when training your dog.

When compared to other domesticated animals, dogs are also more verbally expressive, which adds to their allure.

Understanding these signals and what they mean can be very helpful in understanding dog behavior for effective training, from the whining of puppies to the angry growl of an adult dog. The dog owner should be aware of the noises that express annoyance and how to train the dog to stop making them. Once the verbal expressions are well understood, a dog can be trained to stop barking.

A waggled tail

The position of a dog's tail expresses a lot about the dog's behavior, and the message is the same whether the dog is speaking to a human or another dog. As much as a wagging tail expresses a dog's friendliness, this is not always the case. Dogs have been known to communicate a lot of information through their tails, and not all of it is positive. When you see a dog wagging its tail quickly and widely, it means the dog is pleased to see you and is excited and happy.

If you notice a dog holding its tail loosely but horizontally, this indicates that the dog is curious about you. The dog may not be ready to greet you with a lick, but it will not challenge you either. The same is true for a dog wagging its tail slowly; it's still deciding whether you're a friend or foe. A relaxed dog will keep his tail lowered but not between his legs. Keep an eye out for a dog whose tail is held high and stiff while wagging quickly. The message is that the dog may be aggressive and agitated, and that precautions should be taken to avoid being confronted by the dog.

A cock of the head and a twitch of the ears

Dogs communicate with both ends of their bodies, and a cock of the head or twitch of the dog's ear indicates alertness and interest, though it can also indicate fear at times. When a dog notices something exciting or new, the ears rise or forward, and because canine hearing abilities are quite sharp, a dog will be aware of an approaching car or person when the owner is still a long way away. As a result, dogs are regarded as excellent warning systems because the ears are designed in a way that allows them to focus in different directions, making it easy for the dogs to determine where the noise is coming from.

When a dog's head is down and his ears are back, it indicates that the dog is scared or even submissive. When approaching a dog with this expression, one should proceed with caution. If the dog feels cornered, it has the ability to defend itself by launching an attack.

The instinct of the dog

A dog's instincts make it an excellent observer, capable of paying close attention to everything that happens around them. You may not realize it, but your dog is constantly on the lookout, learning your habits and listening to you. The dog may appear to be reading your mind at times, and its ability to predict every move you make is an expression of good observation skills. When you look at a dog's facial expression, you are more likely to notice some additional clues, such as when you notice a dog pull the corners of the mouth to show teeth; this should not be confused with a raised upper lip with bared teeth as that is a threat gesture, whereas a pull of the corners of the mouth is an expression to other dogs that they do not mean harm.

Body of a dog

A dog's entire body can be used to convey a message at times. Rolling their belly up, exposing the neck, or even the genitals, are all signs that you are the boss. Bowing is a sign of invitation to play some fun games; a dog may even go down on their front paws or bark in order to entice you or another dog to play with them. In such a case, the best response is to play bow back and then pull out the dog's favorite toy.

Backs of dogs and noise

Dogs use their voices to communicate as well. They back up, growl, wine, and howl in order to get their point across.

One of the most common sounds made by dogs is barking. Dogs generally bark to attract attention, to warn of potential danger, and in some cases to express loneliness or boredom. One should be cautious in how they respond to a dog's barking, and if you respond by yelling at them, they will usually assume you are also barking at them. The dog will then assume that barking is acceptable, which may contradict the lesson you want them to learn.

A puppy's first sound is to whine, and their mothers respond by comforting the whining dog. Instead of soothing a whining dog, ignore it until it decides to be quiet. When the dog is quiet, reward it with praise or petting.

A growl is another common dog noise that serves as a warning that the dog is about to attack if the person or thing does not back off. Growling is an aggressive behavior that should never be ignored. Dogs should never be allowed to growl at their owners or anyone else. If your dog is accustomed to growling, you can enlist the help of a behavioral specialist to assess the situation and ensure that things are under control.

Another common noise made by dogs is howling, which can indicate excitement, loneliness, warning, or even desire. Lonely dogs usually howl to see if anyone is nearby. Howling is contagious, and other dogs in the vicinity can join in on the fun.

What you should know before starting to train your dog

There are some things you should be aware of before learning about the tools and procedures for training dogs.

Consider yourself as a dog.

Dogs lack the ability to think abstractly and frequently see things in their present moment and as immediate, which is very different from how humans see things. Dogs have no moral perspective on what they do or do not do, and this serves as the foundation for all of their training, whether through positive training, or reward, correction reinforcement, or anything in between.

Without having to think ahead, the dog's mind normally interprets a sequence of events with an immediate perspective. People, on the other hand, tend to humanize their dogs, causing them to understand pleasure and punishment. What a dog understands better is the effect of an action on the result, and if the result is desirable, it should be repeated. As a result, the fundamental principle that should guide dog training is action and response. Domesticated dogs will always seek to position themselves in the home as part of the park, but in a dog's mind, the other human members of the family are also a park. If you project your position as the family's alpha leader, your dogs will feel secure and confident as well.

Dogs understand human behavior and can read human body language and emotions, and they will always react to an expressed gesture. For example, if a puppy pees on the carpet, they will either express remorse by lowering their head, hiding, or cowering because they can interpret the gesture of anger. Even as you train the dogs on what is right and wrong, it is critical to keep a close eye on them. Monitor the response to the current action, which is why timing, command, and correction are critical.

Recognize that dogs are social by nature and thrive when they interact with humans. What should be clear is that yelling, hitting, or screaming at your dog for bad behavior will not resolve the problem. Similarly, praising and treating the dog well over a good deed may not reinforce the deed in them. As a result, it is critical for the dog trainer to see things through the dog's eyes. The dog's mind is only capable of holding on to reality for a few seconds, and dog behavior is learned by engaging in whatever works to achieve that goal. Dogs, on the other hand, can be conditioned through repetition, resulting in the establishment of a good behavior.

You may be surprised to learn that owning a dog has numerous health benefits.

- Dogs encourage you to exercise - Dogs, like humans, require walks. So, having a furry friend there to encourage you to exercise and go for a walk or run makes the process a lot more exciting and interesting.

- Reduces the risk of heart disease - Believe it or not, having a dog reduces your risk of dying from heart disease.

- A healthier heart - A study followed a group of people who had their first heart attack and found that those who owned a dog had a significantly lower risk of dying simply because they owned a dog.

- Improve your mood - Dogs reduce anxiety and the risk of developing mood disorders.

- Excellent for children - Having a dog in the house reduces the risk of the child developing asthma and allergies, as well as improving the child's socialization.

CONCLUSION

Thank you for persevering through Training Your Own Service Dog. I hope it was informative and that it provided you with all of the tools you need to achieve your objectives, whatever they may be. Service dogs have been around for quite some time.

Few people are aware that they can train their own Service Dog, and many people are taken advantage of. This book, hopefully, will put an end to that. I hope you learned how to determine which Service Dog breed you want and how to train the Service Dog at home for your specific needs.

We hope this book has helped you better understand the unique bond and incredible experience of working with a service dog.

Mostly, you should use common sense and listen to your dog. Also, keep in mind that as your physical needs change, so will your dog's behavior to accommodate your new circumstances.

Finally, if you found this book useful in any way, please leave a review on Amazon!